Zelda,

The Queen of Paris

Zelda,
The Queen of Paris

The True Story of the Luckiest Dog in the World

PAUL CHUTKOW

Illustrations by J.C. Suarès

LYONS PRESS
Guilford, Connecticut
An imprint of Globe Pequot Press

Lyons Press is an imprint of Globe Pequot Press.

Text design: Sheryl Kober
Layout artist: Melissa Evarts
Project editor: Kristen Mellitt
Illustrations © 2012 by J.C. Suarès

Library of Congress Cataloging-in-Publication Data is available on file.

ISBN 978-0-7627-7147-9

Printed in the United States of America

10 9 8 7 6 5 4 3 2 1

for Zelda,
and for all the dogs who love us,
guide us, and help us understand

Contents

Author's Note ix

Part One: India

CHAPTER ONE: Comic Relief 3

CHAPTER TWO: The Honored Guest 14

CHAPTER THREE: Blackmail 27

CHAPTER FOUR: Mirror, Mirror 39

CHAPTER FIVE: The Invisible Cord 54

CHAPTER SIX: A Moveable Feast 68

Part Two: Paris

CHAPTER SEVEN: Ah, Dog 89

CHAPTER EIGHT: Catcher in the Wry 113

CHAPTER NINE: Intruder in the Dust 130

CHAPTER TEN: This Side of Paradise 143

Part Three: California

CHAPTER ELEVEN: Look Homeward, Angel 173

CHAPTER TWELVE: All Good Things 189

Acknowledgments 211

About the Author 212

Author's Note

In India, wild scavenging street dogs are treated as the lowest of the low. Shopkeepers swat them away with brooms. Mothers scream at them and kick them away from their children. Taxi drivers are happy to drive straight at them and even run them down. After a little time in India, you can understand why: These wild street dogs can be mean and vicious, and many of them carry infections and disease, including the deadly rabies virus. Not surprisingly, almost all of these dogs come to a miserable end.

This is the story of one lowly street dog who was determined to do better. Her name was Zelda, and thanks to her boundless courage, humor, and high spirits she was able to win our hearts, escape the streets, and go on to fame and glory as the Queen of Paris. And there was more. From France, Zelda charmed her way to Italy, San Francisco, New York, and even to the dinner table of John Kenneth Galbraith, where tales of Zelda and her magical odyssey reached the heights of Harvard prestige and Kennedy glamour. Jackie Kennedy herself was known to be a Zelda fan.

For all her renown, our little Zelda remained a sweet and humble soul, an ordinary girl with an extraordinary heart. For fourteen years this strange and wonderful dog lit up our lives and taught us beautiful lessons. I hope she will now do the same for you.

Paul Chutkow
Napa, California

Part One: India

CHAPTER ONE

Comic Relief

Zelda's story really begins with Sheela Karintikal.

We were living in India at the time, at 108 Jor Bagh, a quiet residential corner of New Delhi, and Sheela was the rock of our world. She was our cook, our housekeeper, our translator, our emissary to the neighborhood, and soon she would be the nanny to the baby growing inside my beautiful wife, Eda. Sheela was born a poor servant girl, she could barely read or write her name, but she had a magnificent spirit and deep reservoirs of womanly wisdom.

Physically, Sheela was small and plump, with a generous roll of flesh that peeked out from the midriff of her saris, and from her hearty laugh and her easy, gap-toothed grin, you knew she had something very special inside. Sheela was, in fact, a woman of deep religious faith, and whenever she began fretting about her son, Tony, or about her own future once we left India, I would put my arm around her and say, "Don't worry, Sheela. You're in God's pocket. Everything will turn out just fine."

Sheela and Eda made quite a pair. Eda was a blond, blue-eyed nature girl from Albuquerque, New Mexico, and she had a lawyer's mind, a fiercely independent spirit, and, like Sheela, a soft spot for every living creature, from stray dogs to banana slugs. The woman was irresistible. I had arrived in India a committed bachelor, but on my second night in New Delhi, I ran into Eda, and in about three seconds we had fallen in love and married, and here we were starting a family. Call it fate or destiny or karma, but it was as if all the conniving gods and goddesses of India had spotted these two lonely Americans wandering through life and had decided to merrily fling us together, just to see what kind of sparks would fly. And just when our new lives together seemed far too sweet, those same conniving gods sent Zelda down to bite me on the bottom.

Literally.

Every morning, often at first light, when the birds of India bring up the volume on their mesmerizing symphony, this scraggly little street dog would appear at our back door, begging for a morsel of food and a warm, friendly scratch behind her perky puppy ears. One look into her exhausted eyes and you knew she had spent the entire night out on the streets, wandering, dodging trouble, and trying to find something, anything, decent to eat. She was a small dog, about thirty pounds, and she was bone thin, with a black coat that was rust-colored in several places from malnutrition. She was a common street dog, what the Indians call a "pi dog," but her general build and coloring were those of a small black Lab, though her legs and paws were smaller and her muzzle much finer. She also had something unusual on her chest: a small tuft of pure white fur, a genetic gift from parents she probably never knew. And there was something else unique about this dog: No matter how tired or hungry she was, when she appeared at our door, she always came with a smile on her face and a tail waving with excitement and good cheer. Right away you could see it: This dog had dignity; if beg she must, then she would do so with panache and her best paw forward.

Sheela could not resist her. And neither could Eda. Every morning, guided by their tender hearts, they would invite Zelda into the kitchen and offer our scruffy little visitor scraps of meat or a few chapatis, the flat, flavorful Indian breads that Sheela made from scratch. Some mornings Eda and Sheela would offer the dog a bowl of soy milk or some leftover rice and dal, the spicy lentils we loved so much. No matter what was on the menu, the famished beast would scarf it all down, beg for a last scratch of her drooping puppy ears, and then head back out into the streets to look for a safe place to curl up and finally get some sleep.

From the start, this dog had me worried.

She was endearing, to be sure, and though we saw nothing mean or vicious about her, she still had very sharp teeth, and once or twice when I was playing with her, she had nipped my hand and made me bleed. God forbid that should happen to my very pregnant lady; who knew what sort of deadly diseases this wandering mutt might be carrying? Worse still, I could see that this dog had a very strong will and an unpredictable wild streak. She loved to roughhouse, and sometimes when she got excited, she would spin out of all control—and the last thing I wanted was for her to be around a newborn baby. I warned Sheela and Eda about feeding her and keeping her around, but the little dog kept showing up, morning and night, and I knew they must be sneaking her a little food and milk on the side. "Now, Sheela," I would say, feigning a menacing tone. "Yes, Sahib," she would say a little sheepishly, using an Indian term of respect. "No more dog. Baby coming . . ."

Still, I had more pressing things to worry about: I was working for the Associated Press and helping to cover one of the biggest news stories in the world. Indira Gandhi was prime minister, and although India still proudly proclaimed itself to be "the world's largest democracy," she was running the country as if it were her own personal fiefdom and a family dynasty that should never be challenged. But challenged it was. When the nation's highest court found her guilty of several counts of election fraud, Mrs. Gandhi responded by declaring a national emergency, jailing her political opponents, suspending civil liberties, and clamping a heavy lid of censorship on the lively and cantankerous Indian press. With most of her opponents silenced, she then had the Indian Parliament simply erase the election laws that she had been found guilty of violating. Easy as pie.

Almost.

To justify her "National Emergency" and her snuffing of democratic freedoms, Mrs. Gandhi proclaimed to the world that India was besieged by ruthless enemies, both domestic and foreign. To highlight that claim, she had her ministers throw two dozen foreign correspondents out of the country, accusing them, in essence, of being spies and enemies of the state, out to subvert India and ruin its future. This was hogwash, of course, but one of the correspondents tossed out was Ed Cody of the Associated Press. The AP chose me to take

Ed's place. Thus began my first assignment as a foreign correspondent, and thus began, when I was twenty-eight, my firsthand experience of the many veils and deceptions that accompany tyranny and dictatorship.

The work was demanding and nerve-racking. Mrs. Gandhi and India's experiment in dictatorship were front-page news around the world, and there were only a handful of us left in India to cover the story. That meant our dispatches carried enormous weight in foreign capitals and on the scales of world opinion. As a result, the Indian government and its brigade of censors scrutinized every dispatch and every word we wrote, looking for violations of their censorship guidelines—and looking for any excuse to expel us from the country. To that same end, our daily comings and goings were carefully monitored by India's security forces, and Mrs. Gandhi herself kept up the pressure by lashing out in speeches against the CIA, the "evil" Western press, and other dark forces that she claimed were out to destabilize India and tumble her from power. Inside the foreign press corps, we made light of her incessant attacks, but we all knew that we were highly visible targets for expulsion—or worse.

I followed this drama from an ideal perch. The chief of the AP bureau was Myron Belkind, a veteran India hand and one of America's most respected foreign correspondents. Myron handled the lion's share of our political coverage, and that left me free to nose around and write about India's fights against hunger, malaria, smallpox, illiteracy, and chronic economic stagnation. I was also writing about India's attempt to curb its rampant population growth by means of a controversial program of coerced sterilizations. What Myron and I were writing was explosive stuff, and our dispatches were carried in leading newspapers around the world. So Myron and I were under constant scrutiny and pressure.

How did we handle it?

In danger-filled war zones, foreign correspondents are notorious for their partying, carousing, and heavy consumption of alcohol; our group was a shade tamer. The Reuters crew built a badminton court behind their office; they liked to unwind there with round-robin matches. We often joined them. Bill Borders of *The New York Times* and his wife Barbara preferred to invite friends in for cocktails, camaraderie, and superb Indian dinners. For Myron and his lovely Indian wife Rachel, a big night out on the town was steaks at the U.S. Embassy grill and a half bottle of rosé, enough to get them both delightfully tipsy. Vic Vanzi, the UPI man who was there when I arrived, was more old school: He hosted famously drunken parties fueled by cases of his favorite brew, Rosy Pelican, an Indian beer that made the hair on my arms stand up and salute. When John Needham replaced Vic for UPI, the intellectual tenor of the foreign press corps immediately soared, while national sales of Rosy Pelican took a terrible dive. When we wanted peace and quiet, Eda and I would invite John and his wife Chris over for some cut-throat Scrabble or bridge and a dinner featuring Sheela's famous curries, okra, or banana bread. For me, all of these endeavors were relaxing, but when I needed pure comic relief, guess where I found it:

Yup, from that crazy street dog begging at our door.

Lord knows where she spent her daylight hours, but when evening fell, the pup would be back at our kitchen door, batting her eyes at Sheela and playing her like a cello. All of my stern admonitions to Sheela and Eda went for naught; the two of them just couldn't say no to that endearing little dog. Now you can see my predicament: Eda could not resist the dog—and I could not resist Eda, not with those blue eyes and that adventurous spirit of hers. So I began to look for something positive in that dog, some small redeeming virtue in this otherwise wild, mangy, scavenging beast.

One evening when I was especially stressed, I decided to try an experiment. I adore baseball, and growing up, when I could find no one else to play with, I would summon the family dog to play a rousing game of fetch. Might this work with our girl from the streets? I decided to find out. That evening, after Sheela had stuffed her silly with scraps from the table, I grabbed three used tennis balls and lured the puppy out to the small park that wrapped around our house. It was twilight, the ferocious heat of the day was starting to dissipate, and off in a far corner of the park were two huge water buffalo, munching grass and swatting flies with their tails. In the morning they would be busy pulling a heavy metal grass-cutter around the park, but right now they were quiet and mellow, leaving the dog and me plenty of room to play—*if* she'd play.

To start my experiment, I took a tennis ball and waved it under her nose, as if it were an enticing treat. The dog looked at it quizzically, as if she had never even seen a ball before, much less played with one. Then I stood up and sent the ball sailing into the distance, hoping she would go fetch it. But the dog just looked at me as if I were some sort of idiot. So then I took another ball and got down on my knees and rolled it to her. It hit her smack in the nose. She had no idea what to do with it. On my next try, I rolled the ball between her outstretched legs. Now out came one paw, then the other, and soon she was flipping the ball from one paw to the other, like a kid with a soccer ball. Then I quickly snatched the ball away, wound up, and pretended to throw it. The dog stared off into the distance, now eager to give chase. When she turned and saw the ball still in my hand, she got it; she saw I was teasing her. Game on.

Soon she was chasing down the ball and then running back to tease me: She'd refuse to give me the ball back. I was ready for that. I had a chapati in my pocket, and all I had to do was offer her a morsel and she would instantly drop the ball and grab the treat. Then I'd snatch the ball away and we'd start all over. By now we were both having a blast.

We played like that for over an hour, and in my silliness I imagined that I was somehow taming this wild creature, that I was introducing her to the rudiments of canine training. The truth, of course, was that she was training me—and seducing me in the process. That night we stayed out in the park until it was too dark to see, and when I had had enough, I gathered up the tennis balls and waved at her to come in for a final treat. No way. She was loving all the exercise and attention and was in no mood to stop. "Come on, let's go," I called, but she just sat on the grass and refused to budge. "All right," I finally said. "One last throw . . ."

With that, I flung the ball as far as I could and the dog leapt up and went racing after it. She fetched it and came storming back. I offered her a final treat, but she wasn't interested; she wanted more play. When I said no, she dropped the ball and began running in circles around me, barking furiously, nipping at my ankles, and refusing to stop. Around and around me she flew, teasing me, taunting me, goading me to keep on playing. Once or twice I lunged down to grab her, but she was far too quick. Then suddenly she leapt up and bit me on the bottom.

"Ouch!" It hurt, even through my jeans, but the little monster just sat back on her haunches, grinning and just as pleased as she could be.

"So," I said, wagging my finger at her, "you're a wild and crazy girl! With a devilish sense of humor! I think we'd better name you Zelda!"

At this stage, my friends, let me assure you: I had absolutely no intention of adopting this crazy street dog. Play ball with her? Sure. Bring her into the family? No way. Completely out of the question. Now don't get me wrong: I love dogs. When I was growing up outside of Chicago, we always had dogs in the house, and I loved playing with them, teaching them tricks, taking them on hikes, and having them sleep at my feet on cold winter nights. But this little monster was a whole other matter. We couldn't take her in: She was too wild, too zany, and potentially too dangerous. Still, that pain in my rear dictated what I had to do next: I had to find a veterinarian and get this beast a rabies shot. If she was going to hang around our door, we had to be extra careful, especially with Eda being pregnant and the baby coming. Eda and Sheela immediately agreed: Better to be safe than sorry. Little did we know, though, what that simple rabies shot would soon entail . . .

CHAPTER TWO

The Honored Guest

My favorite taxi driver in India was Punjab Singh.

Punjab was a sprightly Sikh gentleman with a white beard and a faded red turban, and he had about two teeth left in his mouth. What he had lost in teeth, though, Punjab had gained in worldly wisdom. He was a sage and a philosopher, and I loved to take him with me on my reporting trips, both to translate and to help me understand the situation from his own special point of view. For instance, when the monsoons came and the Jumna River flooded, it was Punjab who went with me to inspect the damage and help interview the afflicted families. And when I had clandestine meetings with an elderly Indian couple who were organizing political resistance to Mrs. Gandhi, it was Punjab I relied upon to drive me to their neighborhood and drop me off a safe distance away. I never gave him their exact address, not because I didn't trust him but because I wanted to shield him from scrutiny or having to lie to authorities on my behalf.

Naturally, then, on that morning when Eda and I outfitted Zelda with a new collar and leash and got her ready for her debut in civilized society, it was Punjab Singh I asked for when I called the Jor Bagh taxi stand. Luckily for me, Punjab was not out on a call, and a few minutes later he pulled up to our front gate, his black taxi with the yellow roof looking almost as old and weathered as he did. "Good morning, Sahib," he said. "And where is it that we shall be going this morning?"

Then I brought Zelda up to his cab, and a strange look came across Punjab's face, as if I had totally lost my mind. "We, sir," I said, "are going to the stables of the president of India!"

Punjab cocked his head in silent assent and opened the door for me and the beast. On the backseat I spread out an old towel that I had brought for the purpose, and then I coaxed Zelda in and sat down beside her. Then off we went. Punjab, I'm sure, was dismayed at having this uncouth street dog in the back of his taxi, but he had the good grace to discuss only the heat. "Very hot," I said.

"Like an inferno, Sahib. Even at night. Very, very hard to sleep."

Why were we headed for the president's stables? Well, the morning before, I had gone to see my pal Bill Borders over at the New Delhi office of *The New York Times*. Bill had arrived in India a few weeks before I had, and he had brought with him a colorful entourage: his wife Barbara, their five-year-old son Willy, and a fun, droopy-eyed basset hound named Ratchet. The *Times* office was only a short walk from our AP bureau, but by the time I got there, I was drenched in sweat. I collapsed in front of Bill's desk, and Anthony, the *Times* office manager, brought me a Coke. "Really, Paul," Bill said, "you should not be out jogging when it's 116 in the shade."

Bill was a fellow midwesterner, born and bred in St. Louis, and he had a natural wit and graciousness that his postings in Africa and Canada had done nothing to sully. "Now," Bill said, "something tells me that you're here for some very important matter. Otherwise you'd simply phone . . ."

"You're right, sir," I said. "I am here on a subject of paramount importance. Never mind Indira Gandhi. Never mind this foul 'National Emergency' of hers. I have come here to ask you about your boy Ratchet. He seems in fine form. What do you do for a vet?"

Bill laughed. "Oh, I really couldn't say . . ."

"What do you mean?"

"Well, I'm way too embarrassed to tell you."

"Come on now, William. I'll throw in lunch if I have to."

"Well, please don't tell anyone, but Ratchet goes to what is surely the most exclusive and most expensive vet on the Asian subcontinent. The one who takes care of the horses of the president of India. You know, those beautiful thoroughbreds that draw the presidential carriage . . ."

"Well, well, well, the president's vet. I *am* impressed."

Bill was now very intrigued. "But tell me, Paul, why in the world do you need a vet? Eda's not having puppies, is she?"

"Well, now I am the one who's embarrassed . . ."

At this point I told Bill the story of Zelda, the crazy street dog, and he was very amused. And I think he took particular pleasure in imagining me showing up at the presidential stables with a foul little pooch in tow. "Well, my friend," he said, "your solution is named Dr. Karb. He costs a fortune, but the man is marvelous. It's a little hard to get to see him, though. I had to pull a few strings . . ."

So much in India, from the critical to the mundane, involved "pulling a few strings." When I first arrived and needed a phone at home, Myron, as chief of the AP bureau, had to write a formal letter to the director of the PTT, the department of the Post, Telephone & Telegraph, explaining my need and seeking a formal waiver from the usual delay in obtaining a phone. Then I had to go in person to the PTT to prove my bona fides to the director himself. In his office, I sat around a large table with twenty other supplicants, each of us desiring to be honored with the privilege of having a phone. All the others, apart from me, had brought with them a special offering for the director: a wreath of flowers with an envelope tucked inside, a book wrapped with an effusive bow and an envelope inside, or a box of chocolates—again with an envelope discreetly placed inside. All of those envelopes contained, of course, vast sums of rupees, which the director sweetly thought of as "gratuities" but which everyone else called *baksheesh*—a little oil to grease the wheels of bureaucracy. In an environment of such commonplace corruption, I wondered what it would take to secure an audience with the veterinarian of the president of India.

To my surprise, with just one phone call Bill was able to smooth the way: Dr. Karb's office set me up with an appointment for the very next morning. And now here I was, in the back of Punjab Singh's taxi, headed for the presidential stables—and feeling very uneasy about the trip. For her debut in Indian society, Eda and I had outfitted Zelda with a sparkling new collar of red and green plaid—in our rush, it was the only one we could find—but to me it looked ridiculous, like placing a jeweled tiara on the head of a frog. And what if this beast badly misbehaved? What then?

Still, Zelda was now sitting primly beside me. Had she ever ridden in a car before? Did she somehow sense she was on an important outing? I could only guess.

On the outskirts of town, Punjab turned onto a country road lined with tall, stately trees and flanked on either side by acres of green fields, now resplendent in the morning sun. Punjab let out a long, low whistle. On our right were dozens of horses going through their morning workouts, under the watchful eyes of a whole team of trainers. The horses themselves were magnificent, their necks long and regal, their manes elegantly braided, their heads noble and a little haughty, as befit their caste and presidential status. In the distance we could see the stables, their white façades freshly scrubbed, and on the roof was a golden weather vane, polished to a shine. "So much money for horses," Punjab sighed, "and so little for people . . ." Now you know why I loved the guy.

At the entrance to the stables was a guardhouse and gate. A Sikh soldier flagged us to a halt and asked Punjab the nature of our visit. Then he cast a dubious eye at the cargo in the back. Finally, he waved us through. In a corner of the stable area, beside a row of chain-link dog runs, we found the headquarters of Dr. Karb. Punjab parked a discreet distance away, and then I straightened Zelda's collar and smoothed her coat, as if a final touch-up could somehow turn this lowly mutt into something less than a complete embarrassment. Zelda then hopped out of the taxi and immediately relieved herself on an artfully sculpted bush. Well, I thought, this is going to be interesting.

The clinic inside was neat and clean and smelled of bleach. There was no waiting area; it was one large room, and as soon as I walked in, Dr. Karb himself waved from across the room. Then he wiped his hands and hurried over. He was a congenial man, dressed in crisp khaki shorts and a shirt, and he greeted me with a sturdy handshake. He was very British in his manner, as many upper-class Indians tend to be. Splendid chap. Then he looked down and saw Zelda. "This?" he said. "This?"

"Yes, this . . ."

"I am so very sorry," he said. "She has bitten someone, hasn't she?"

"No, no. I've just come to get her a rabies shot. Preventively."

Dr. Karb knelt down beside Zelda, lifted her lips back to inspect her gums and teeth, and then ran his hand from her neck down to her haunches. Then he stood up. "Mr. Chutkow, this is a common pi dog, a wild beast that has been roaming the streets and eating garbage."

"Yes, I know that."

"My dear fellow," Dr. Karb said, in an almost brotherly way, "we can find you a proper dog. A King Charles spaniel, a German pointer, or perhaps a fine rottweiler. A dog with correct manners and breeding."

"Well," I said, "this one *does* have a wonderful sense of humor . . ."

"Mr. Chutkow, I must say that a dog like this can be very dangerous and may do to you many things that you will not find the slightest bit funny."

Now I was at a loss for words. I wanted to explain to him that my wife was pregnant, that I didn't really want to adopt the dog, just get her a rabies shot, but I feared he'd find that insulting. Dr. Karb was, after all, in charge of some of the most prized animals in the world, and here I was bringing him a pariah from the streets. What had I been thinking? This was, I now could see, an appalling waste of this good man's time.

Then it happened.

As I fumbled for words, Zelda stood up on her hind legs and gave Dr. Karb's hand a friendly nuzzle. His first instinct was to pull back, but Zelda stayed on her hind legs, nudging his hand, until Dr. Karb reached down and scratched her ears, just the way she loved. Then she lunged up to kiss his face, even as he tried to hold her away. "All right," he said. "Let's put her up on the table and have a closer look."

Dr. Karb hoisted Zelda onto his examining table and began poking around. "No tumors. No cysts. Her puppy teeth are gone. I'd say she's about ten months old. Maybe a year. Have you given her a name?"

"Yes, we call her Zelda."

Dr. Karb laughed. "Ah, crazy Zelda Fitzgerald! Read F. Scott in school. First-rate stuff. And you are a journalist, am I hearing correctly?"

"Yes, guilty as charged."

"Well, one day we must chat more about that, but what exactly is it that you want me to do with this . . . this little pi dog?"

"Just a rabies shot, please, and then we'll be on our way."

"I am so sorry, Mr. Chutkow, but I cannot possibly give this dog a rabies shot."

"Really? Why not?"

"Because it will kill her. Her body is too weak to support it."

"Well, she seems pretty strong to me . . ."

"Okay," Dr. Karb said. "I will try to explain. Yes, she looks strong. But—and pardon me for asking—have you ever seen this dog poop?"

"Well, yes."

"The result is not pretty, is it?"

"Uh, no. Definitely not."

"You see, Mr. Chutkow, dogs like this always have worms and parasites, many different varieties of them. And look at her coat. It's disgusting. And I can assure you that her coat and skin are filled with many, many things that you do not want to touch. You don't let her inside the house, do you?"

"Well, no, of course not," I lied.

"Good! And please tell me there are no babies in your home."

"Oh no. No babies," I said. I didn't dare tell him about the one on the way.

"Well," Dr. Karb said, "thank heaven for that!"

I reached out to Zelda and scratched her ears as she stood on Dr. Karb's table. *Well, kid,* I thought. *That's it . . .*

"Mr. Chutkow," he said, "I can see you are an admirable chap, wanting to save a poor street dog like this. But I must highly recommend that you send her on her way. Better yet, leave her here with us and we will dispose of her in a very kindly manner."

Dispose of her? What a pleasant way to put it . . .

"Mr. Chutkow, I am sorry. I'm afraid there is nothing more I can do for your little friend." Then he saw my hand stroking her face. "Unless . . ."

"Unless?"

"Well, if you really want, I suppose we could try to deworm her. It would take several treatments, but we could give it a try. And we could try cortisone shots to build up her strength and her immune system."

"Would that work?"

"I can make no promises."

"And her coat? What could we do with that?"

"Well, we could give her daily medicinal baths for a week or two, to clean up her coat and kill the underlying parasites. But this would take time and be a very expensive proposition. And if she wanders back onto the street, she would be right back where she started. Not an auspicious prospect, I'm afraid."

Okay, the heck with this, I thought; I've done all I can. It wasn't the money that was too costly, it was the time and effort. I was already working ten or twelve hours a day, oftentimes more, and Eda was too, handling some local manufacturing problems for Esprit, the fashion company based in San Francisco. Most important, India was now major international news, and Myron and the AP deserved my full energy and attention. Getting this dog fixed up would take weeks and weeks and be a monstrous diversion; how in the world could I justify that?

"Thank you, Dr. Karb," I said. "This just isn't going to work . . ."

"Mr. Chutkow, I must say you make a wise decision. Shall we handle it from here?"

"Maybe tomorrow. Can I pay you something for your time?"

"Heavens no, sir. It has been both my duty and my privilege."

Dr. Karb lifted Zelda up off the table and set her down on the floor; I prayed she wouldn't squat down and pee right there. Or worse. Through the door I could see Punjab Singh waiting outside. Then Zelda looked up at me as if to say, "So that's it? You're giving up on me? You're putting me back out on the street?"

"Shut up, you," I said silently and led her out the door. At that same sculpted bush, Zelda squatted down again, as if to show me just how polite and mannerly she could be. And as I swooped her up and got ready to toss her back into Punjab's taxi, I felt a sharp pang inside my chest. "No, Paul," I told myself. "Don't do this. Please. Think of Eda. Think of the baby on the way. Remember, better safe than sorry, right?" Then Zelda climbed up onto my thighs, and what remained of my sanity instantly melted away. I took the dog in my arms and lifted her right up to my face: "If you make me regret this, I swear I will wring your bloody little neck! Do you understand me? Do you, you little monster?" Zelda now nuzzled my cheek, as sweetly as she could.

With that, I marched her right back in to Dr. Karb. He was only mildly surprised to see us. "Well," I said, "I've done a lot of foolish things in my life, but probably none quite as foolish as this. When can we start?"

"Right away, my friend. You leave her with us. We will give her a special bath and a cortisone shot, then we will test her blood and urine and watch her through the night. By tomorrow morning we should know where we stand."

"That sounds fine. Thank you, Dr. Karb. Please treat her well . . ."

"Of course, Mr. Chutkow. Now she will be our honored guest."

I just smiled. Zelda had gone from pariah to honored guest in what seemed the blink of an eye. She was obviously a very special girl.

From outside, Punjab Singh had watched this entire scene unfold, and when I came back to his taxi he opened the rear door for me with a bemused twinkle in his eye. "Home, Sahib? Or we go to office?"

"Oh, I don't know. The office, I guess."

For a long time we rode in silence. Then Punjab let out a wistful sigh. "Life, Sahib, it is a great mystery. All we can do is follow our heart."

CHAPTER THREE

Blackmail

In India, we had terrorists right in our front yard.

They hid in the trees, keeping us under constant surveil-
lance. Then, if we turned our backs for only a second, they
would swoop down and launch their attack. At first, our terrorists would content themselves with snatching our breakfast
toast or a scrap of muffin. But when Zelda returned to us from
Dr. Karb and was staying with us for the course of her treat-
ment, she became their favorite target, and our terrorist crows
devised the most cunning ways to tease and torment her.

One evening, for instance, Eda and I were out on the front porch before dinner, watching the light recede and enjoying the first breaths of relief from the excruciating heat of the day. Then out came Sheela with a plate of freshly made *papadum*, those crispy Indian chips that are marvelous appetizers, especially when served with a lime soda or something stiffer. Zelda looked annoyed: What, no appetizer for me? So I went into the kitchen to see what I could find for our hungry little girl.

There was no shortage of treats in the refrigerator. In addition to her daily regimen of cortisone shots and medicinal baths, Zelda had been put on a diet rich in protein, to help her gain strength and repair her coat. So two or three times a week, Sheela was going to the butcher in Jor Bagh and coming back home with all sorts of meats for us—and for Zelda. Then Sheela would cook several days' worth of food for the dog, adding in rice, vegetables, and healthy remnants from our dinners and lunches. Sheela went to great lengths to fatten up her pal Zelda, but she was also a little dismayed. "You know, Memsahib," she said one day to Eda, "this dog eats better than most people in India."

Spare ribs, we discovered, were Zelda's favorite. Sheela had a wonderful way of cooking pork ribs for us, with soy sauce and Indian spices, and she would mix some of the meat into Zelda's food as well. Then for days afterward we had special treats for Zelda: hardened rib bones for her to chew, under our watchful eye, of course. Now, as dinner approached, I found a stash of rib bones in the refrigerator and brought one out for Zelda. And as soon as she was stretched out on the lawn with her bone between her paws, those evil crows hatched their plot and swung into action.

We didn't spot them up in the trees, waiting for the moment to strike, but what followed was very cleverly conceived and executed. First, one of the crows began cackling wildly, snaring our attention and Zelda's, too. Then the crow flattened back its wings and did a dive-bomb straight for Zelda's head. Zelda leapt to her feet, ready to fend off the attack. But the crow skidded away with a delirious shriek and Zelda chased it to the top of the bushes on the far side of the yard. From there, the crow lazily flew up and resumed his position in the trees, gazing back down with a most satisfied air. When Zelda returned for her bone, of course it was gone; a second crow, working in tandem, had sneaked in and snatched it away when no one was looking. Zelda put her nose to the ground and scoured the lawn for her missing treasure, but it was nowhere to be found. Then she looked back at us with baleful eyes; our girl had been thoroughly had.

No worries, though. I went into the kitchen and came back with another rib bone for Zelda's amusement—and for ours. This was terrific entertainment. Our front porch usually was. Sitting there, morning or night, was like having front-row seats at an Indian version of Barnum & Bailey; a stream of exotic acts was always parading by. There was the tall, statuesque lady who sold us mangoes from the huge basket she carried atop her head. There was the old man with the flute who carried a cobra in a hooded basket and for five rupees would make him dance. There was the ragged, barefoot boy who led his camel through the streets of Jor Bagh on a tattered rope, calling all the kids to come out for a ride. And then there was our *chowkidar*, the neighborhood watchman who every night would pass by on his appointed round, tapping on our gate with his wooden stick, just to let us know that all was well. Tonight, at the very first tap, Zelda rushed over to greet him—giving those evil crows ample time to swoop down and snatch her second bone. Our girl had been had again.

We had another miscreant in our neighborhood, and this one was not as cunning or amusing as our terrorist crows. He was the chauffeur for one of our neighbors, a doctor, and the chauffeur and his family lived in the servants' quarters in the alleyway behind our house. One night, as Zelda was finishing her treatments from Dr. Karb, Eda and I were having dessert on the porch when Sheela suddenly appeared from the kitchen. "Problem, Sahib. Chauffeur wants to see you."

Sheela led the man out onto the porch, and with an accusatory tone he launched into a tirade in Hindi that neither Eda nor I could decipher. As always, Sheela came to the rescue. "He says Jelda is his dog." (Sheela never could get that "Z" in Zelda right.) "He calls her Blackie and says he feeds her every day. Sahib, he says you steal his dog."

Steal, eh?

At this stage, we had a substantial investment in Zelda. Most trips to our own doctor, Duke Chawla, a Harvard-trained specialist in tropical medicine, cost us the equivalent of about $8, but at Dr. Karb's clinic, Zelda had run up a tab fifteen or twenty times as great, a lot of money for a beast from the street. More important, we had grown attached to this little monster. Still, we had made no decision to adopt her; in my mind we were just rehabilitating her so that we could then go about finding her a proper home with an Indian family. Nonetheless, I was not about to be conned into letting her go, and certainly not by this chap. His motives were clearly suspect. I had no trouble believing that Zelda had been spreading her charms around the neighborhood, the adorable little trollop, but I had plenty of trouble believing that this fellow cared one whit about the dog. My guess was that he had spotted Zelda in our yard, had seen the affection we had developed for her, and had then, like our terrorist crows, concocted his scheme. His claim of ownership, I felt sure, was nothing more than a shakedown mission—and I was having none of it.

"So," I said to the man, "you say we have stolen your dog, is that correct?" Sheela translated and he immediately nodded his assent.

"Okay!" I said, standing up. "Then we must call the police! I'll go get the phone."

This time there was no need for Sheela to translate; the man knew plenty of English, enough anyway. "Wait!" he said. "No police!"

Before I left for India, Stan Swinton, the head of the AP's World Services and a legendary foreign correspondent, took me out to lunch and told me everything he thought I needed to know about India and my first foreign assignment. "India is going to shock you to the core," Stan said. "It is going to challenge every fiber of your being and every belief you've ever had about democracy and dictatorship, about what is moral and what is not. Just remember this: Your job as a correspondent is not to judge; it is to understand."

Stan was right: Almost every day in India brought some new shock, some new moral dilemma for us to confront and try to understand. For instance, once I had found the house to rent in Jor Bagh, Myron told me I had to set about the task of hiring a staff: a cook, a woman to sweep the floors, a laundryman, and more. "Myron," I said, "I don't want all that. I

don't want servants of any sort! I can do everything myself."
Myron just laughed. "First of all," he said, "you won't have
the time or the energy to do *anything* for yourself. We have
a huge story to cover. When are you going to have time to
shop for food or do laundry—in one-hundred-plus-degree
heat? Besides, this is India; if you don't hire servants, your
neighbors will take it as an insult—they'll say you're refusing
to support their people."

From there, the moral complexities only deepened.
My new landlady begged me to hire her laundryman, her
dhobi, arguing that he was dirt poor and with a wife and
baby he desperately needed the money. So I interviewed her
dhobi and hired him on the spot. He was terribly shy and
painfully thin, with legs like toothpicks, and the little vest
he wore hung on his chest like it might on a cadaver. Right
away, though, the dhobi and I became great pals. When he
arrived on his bicycle two mornings a week, we would laugh
and kid each other—even though we couldn't understand a
word the other said. The dhobi was a jewel: He had soul, he
had a playful sense of humor, and he seemed to carry the
weight of the world on his frail little shoulders. I called him
"Dhobi Dubinsky, the only Jewish laundryman in the whole
of India."

By his fourth week on the job, I felt so bad for the dhobi
that I doubled his salary. I thought I was doing the right

thing. But as soon as she heard this news, our landlady stormed down from her apartment upstairs and began to bellow. "You have no idea what you have done!" she cried. Yes, she had insisted I hire her dhobi because he was so poor, but now I was paying him far too much—I was going to spoil him and ruin everything for her and everyone else in Jor Bagh! Mark Twain would have found this scene delicious: We were the perfect innocents abroad.

Then there was the fateful case of Romboli. When Eda and I first set up the house in Jor Bagh, we had a lovely sweeper girl named Lalita. She came to the house morning and evening, and she would get down on her haunches and crawl, crablike, through the house, sweeping up the dirt and dust with a primitive hand broom made of straw. When Lalita was sent off to get married—I think she was about twelve years old—Sheela found us Romboli, a poor woman, much older, whose saris were faded and ripped and who carried about her a palpable air of bitterness and resentment. Romboli was with us for only a few weeks when I started to wonder if something was amiss.

Eda and I were usually having breakfast on the front porch when Romboli arrived, and my wallet would usually be left on our nightstand, back in our bedroom. One day, when I got ready to leave for the office, I found my wallet was rather thin; I had fewer rupees than I remembered. I did not pay it much mind—the sum involved amounted to only a few dollars—but when this kept recurring, I voiced my suspicions to Eda and Sheela. Eda, being a lawyer, wanted proof. Sheela, having hired Romboli and feeling responsible to us, wanted justice. So we put secret markings on all of my bills, and the next morning, when several rupees again disappeared from my wallet, Sheela sprang into action. She confronted Romboli and even searched her sari. When the marked rupees were discovered, Sheela was livid, and a few minutes later we were all crowded into a taxi and headed for Romboli's house, to recover more of her loot.

Romboli and her young daughter, we discovered, did not live in servants' quarters; they lived in a crumbling shantytown, in a hovel with flattened cardboard boxes for walls, a broken *charpoi* on which to sleep, and a pile of dirty clothes stuffed in a corner. On our high-minded quest for justice, we made Romboli pull out from under her charpoi a small chest, fixed with a lock. Burning with shame, Romboli opened it. Inside was a thick wad of rupees, all in small denominations, maybe $30 or $40 in total. Suddenly I felt sick. What in the world were we doing? Humiliating this poor woman in front of her neighbors, retrieving her illgotten gains? For God's sake, if I were living in that hovel and trying to feed my child, I'd steal a few rupees here and there too, especially from a careless American too stupid to put away his wallet. So in the end we took no money back from Romboli; I even gave back to her what she had stolen from us, plus a little extra, on the condition that she never return to our home again. Yes, Stan Swinton had been right: Each day in India was a challenge to our values and our habitual ways of thinking; each day was a challenge not to judge but to understand.

Which brings us back to the chauffeur. Suddenly it hit me: Wasn't he just another version of Romboli, seeing in our growing attachment to Zelda an opportunity to slip a little cash from our wallets, cash he may well have needed to feed his wife and children? "So," I said to the man, "you say I stole your dog, but you don't want me to call the police. And I say the dog is ours. So what do you propose we do?"

The chauffeur shifted his weight from one leg to the other and shrugged his shoulders. Then he looked to Sheela, but she wasn't about to give him any comfort. Nor was I. Still, this con man was forcing our hand; the moment of truth was now upon us. So I turned to Eda: "We need to make a decision. Are we going to keep this bloody dog or not?"

Eda turned to Zelda. "Well," she said, "just look at her . . ."

Zelda at that moment was lying on the grass, with her face on her paws and her eyes locked on us. Not once had she deigned to approach the chauffeur, her purported rescuer from the streets of India. Zelda's eyes left us no room for doubt: Our fate was sealed; she was ours to keep. But what to do with this scheming chauffeur? Frankly, I wanted to wring his neck, but as a guest in India I knew that diplomacy was the best and wisest course. And in this case, diplomacy meant only one thing: cold, hard cash. I figured about $20 should do the trick; that was probably more than he made in a week. "Sheela, please tell this fellow I am prepared to offer him 200 rupees for the dog—unless he prefers I call the police "

Sheela was not so generous. After a brief exchange with the man in Hindi, she said, "Give him 150 rupees, Sahib, and then he will be on his way." Then she turned to the chauffeur: "Isn't it?" I had to smile: "Isn't it?" was one of my favorite Indian expressions, and from Sheela's lips it conveyed a marvelous, almost judicial finality.

The chauffeur nodded, averting his eyes, and took the cash. Happily, we never saw hide or hair of him again. And dear Zelda, of course, was now fully and officially ours, for richer, for poorer, in sickness and in health, and for as long as the little devil might live.

And a devil she remained. From that point forward, we made Zelda part of our family. We set her up with a doggie bed and feeding bowls, and we even made up an ID tag with her name and our phone number on it. But none of this settled her down or curbed her nightly bursts of craziness. Out in the park, she still loved to play ball and, at the end of our session, she still loved to leap up and nip me on the bottom—and no warnings or threats could ever dampen her fun. And by now she had developed a far more vexing habit. Once back inside, she would tear through the house, going room to room, and she would always wind up on our bed, spinning in circles, barking with joy, and bunching up our sheets and covers until they were left in a miserable heap. She had spirit, I'd give her that, but now the task at hand was both urgent and essential: This wild beast had to be tamed— and right now, before the baby arrived.

But how in the world were we going to accomplish that?

CHAPTER FOUR

Mirror, Mirror

In our bedroom, we had an unusual resident: a gecko.

I spotted it one morning, hiding behind a large Matisse print that I had treasured since college. By my eye, geckos are not the most attractive creatures on this planet, and finding it gave me a creepy feeling: How dare it invade the intimacy of our bedroom! My first inclination was to capture the intruder and turn it loose outside. But when I went to Sheela for her advice, she was adamant: "Leave it alone, Sahib. Gecko means good luck coming."

I am not, by temperament or training, a superstitious man. As a boy, I loved math and science; I liked their clarity and precision, and I felt comforted by the idea that the mysteries of the universe might one day be solved by penetrating minds and the methodologies of scientific inquiry. I considered myself a man of reason, not of faith or emotion, and when I entered Johns Hopkins University, I did so with the intent of becoming an aerospace engineer and working for NASA. Even when I was bitten by the writing bug and changed my major to the Writing Seminars, I was not drawn to poetry or creative whimsy; I was drawn to journalism, to the systematic marshaling of facts, analyses, and differing points of view. I felt it was my obligation to bring reason and a calm, detached scientific eye to the daily chaos of human events and to covering the news.

India operates on a whole other plane.

India is a land of mystery, a land of arcane gods and cults, of strange rituals and swarming emotions, a land where astrologers, fortune-tellers, palm readers, and seers are never dismissed as kooks or shysters; instead they are embraced and consulted by the highest authorities in the land. Mrs. Gandhi, for one, never made an important decision without first consulting her astrologers, to see if the planets were aligned in favor of her intended action. I tried to resist, but Eda and I were swept up in the swirl.

Before Eda and I got married, Sheela urged us to consult an astrologer and have our charts done, to make sure our astral paths were moving in harmony, both with each other and with the larger movements of the universe. My scientific turn of mind recoiled at the idea, but I nonetheless felt relief when our astrologer inspected our charts and pronounced us fit to be married.

But that was just the beginning. Now that Eda was pregnant, we entered a whole new level of astral speculation. Eda and I are both very private people, but our pregnancy became a very public event, in Jor Bagh and far beyond. Now everyone we knew or met seemed to be in a search for hidden signs and omens, for metaphysical clues as to the gender of our future offspring. Our friends, our neighbors, our taxi drivers, and of course Sheela and her pals were all hunting for signs that pointed to just one happy outcome: "Sahib, Memsahib, we know it for sure: You will be having a son!" Personally, Eda and I had no preference: a boy or a girl would have been equally fine with us. In India and most of Asia, though, having a son is considered the highest of honors and the richest of gifts, an event to be prayed for, and everyone we knew was hoping for a boy. In Sheela's mind, I'm sure that the appearance of that gecko in our bedroom meant, without a shadow of a doubt, that a son was on the way.

Whether it was to be a boy or a girl, one thing was plain for all of us to see: A profound transformation came over Eda while she was pregnant. Before, she had been a beautiful woman; pregnant, she was absolutely radiant. She literally glowed with health and vitality, with energy and joy. Even when she carried a huge balloon-like bulge in her tummy, Eda merrily played tennis and softball and often went swimming at the U.S. Embassy pool. And when NBC Radio was looking for a stringer in India, Eda landed the job and did it with aplomb, pregnancy and all. In my eyes, she was Wonder Woman, with a spirit of adventure that few others could match.

Throughout the first stages of Eda's pregnancy, everything went as we had hoped. But late in the pregnancy, her doctor, an Indian woman trained in London, delivered us some disconcerting news: The baby was breach; he or she was not moving into proper position for delivery. If the baby did not turn over, the doctor warned, the birth might require a cesarean section, and that could be dangerous. To remedy the situation, the doctor urged Eda to stay flat on her back for several weeks, with the bed tilted up at the foot. The idea was that gravity would naturally draw the baby up into the womb and give it more room to turn over and move into proper position.

This approach made me queasy. Where was the science? Where was the sonogram to peer in and see how the baby was doing? Also, if the baby had to be delivered by cesarean, would the clinic in New Delhi have the necessary equipment? Would there be an incubator for the baby, should one be needed? At that time, India was not as advanced as it is today, and I did not like the answers I was hearing. So when the baby refused to turn over, I suggested to Eda that we get on a plane and fly to Bangkok, where we knew there were well-equipped hospitals and clinics.

"Don't be silly," Eda said. "I feel wonderful and everything's going to be fine. After all, millions of women in India have healthy babies every single day, right at home or out in the fields." That was Eda at her finest: fearless, positive, unshakeable in spirit. In sum, magnificent.

And then there was Zelda.

By this time, thanks to Dr. Karb's treatments and Sheela's cooking, Zelda was in tip-top form, physically. She had put on weight, she'd had her rabies shot, those telltale rust blotches had disappeared, and her coat was now luxuriously thick and black. Like Eda, Zelda was now brimming with energy and vitality—and that's exactly where the problem lay.

As the baby's due date approached, the epicenter of our lives shifted from the front porch back to our bedroom. And the room itself was now totally transformed. Against the far wall, we had put in a single bed, where Eda spent most of her time reclining with her legs up, per doctor's orders. In the front of the room, to the side, we had put in a beautiful wicker baby bed, with a colorful mobile that hung from an arm above, its toys dancing happily under the breeze of our ceiling fan. Beside the baby bed, and beside the Matisse print where our gecko lived, we had put in a long, full-length mirror, reaching right down to the floor. Here Eda would regularly stand and examine herself, to see how her body was responding to each phase of the pregnancy. In the center of the room was our king-size bed, which, as we envisioned it, would serve as our feeding station, changing table, and lullaby central once the baby arrived.

Zelda, though, had very different ideas.

The more time we spent in the bedroom, the more possessive Zelda became about "her" bed. When Eda was flat on her back on the single bed, Zelda would spread out on the master bed and occupy it, the way a Prussian general might occupy a newly conquered town. Sometimes as I approached, Zelda would even growl at me, as if I were invading a terrain that belonged entirely to her. Now, as any dog trainer will tell you, these were all signs of dominance, of the dog's insistence that she was in full command. Fine. I get it. But the real question, the question that took on urgent importance as the day of the birth drew near, was: What the heck do we do about it? Break her of the habit? And if so, how?

Now, a skilled dog handler would surely have a solution. And a gifted dog whisperer could probably come in, tune in to Zelda's unusual psyche, and quickly master the situation. I did not fit either description. And I had no time to spend looking for an expert in dog behavior. By this time, Indira Gandhi had done something that none of us had expected: She had called for new elections, designed to legitimize her authoritarian grip on power. Immediately our workload in the AP bureau had doubled. So I was now swamped and had very little time to spend trying to train Zelda or break her of her dangerous habit of taking control of our bed.

Still, something had to be done, and I decided to approach the problem in a rational, scientific way. I laid down a two-pronged strategy: find an effective way to keep Zelda off the bed and, at the same time, teach her to obey basic commands like "Sit!" "Lie down!" and "Speak!" That sort of training, I reasoned, would re-assert my role as the master of the house, the leader of the pack, and, I hoped, it would start to bring this wild beast under control. The strategy made perfect sense, did it not?

To execute my plan, every morning at the crack of dawn I would arm myself with a slew of biscuits or bits of toast and begin the training process. "Zelda, sit!" I would say, and the dog would just stare at me with a blank expression. I would hold the treat high and back over her head, in theory to push her bottom down into a sitting position, but she would just stiffen her legs and leap up for the treat. At times, I would even push her butt down to the floor and reward her, as if she had finally understood the command "Sit!" Still, as hard as I tried, Zelda was never able to connect the word "sit" to the actual act of sitting. My training effort went on like this for days on end and many nights, too. Nothing worked. In the end, I concluded that the word and concept of "obey" were simply not in this wild dog's DNA.

Then there was the issue of the bed. I do not believe in hitting dogs or children, except in extreme cases where issues of safety trump all else. But I was reaching the end of my rope when it came to Zelda and the bed. I would shout "No!" and chase her off the bed and out of the room, but a few minutes later she would sneak right back in and jump aboard. It was exasperating, to say the least. Someone suggested that I use a rolled-up newspaper to discipline her, first by smacking it against my hand—the sound alone would tell her I meant business—and if that didn't work, I should use the paper to whack her across the bottom. In my desperation, I tried both approaches, but this produced no breakthroughs either. I began to think that once the baby arrived, we would have no choice: We would have to ban Zelda from the house and send her back to the streets. What else could we do?

When I was at my wit's end, something very funny happened. One night when Eda and I were getting ready for bed,

Zelda marched in and happened to catch sight of her own reflection in our full-length mirror. Instantly she jumped straight up in shock: What was *that*? You could almost see the question form inside her head. Then she very gingerly approached the mirror again—and when that other dog appeared once more, Zelda jumped back and began barking at it in a frightened, panicky way. Eda and I were hysterical with laughter. This went on for a good twenty minutes, with Zelda sneaking from around the corner to see if the other dog was still there, then jumping back in total bewilderment. She sniffed the floor, she sniffed the wall, she looked under the bed, searching for some clue about this new intruder, but this only tripled her confusion.

Finally Zelda got an idea into her head. She gathered up her courage, got down on all fours, and then slowly crawled right up to the mirror. When the two dogs were nose to nose, Zelda cocked her head—and was delighted that the other dog responded in kind. Then Zelda put one paw up to the glass, and sure enough, the other dog put hers up to greet it. It was touching to watch. Finally, her tail wagging with hope, Zelda inched up to the mirror and gave her new friend an affectionate kiss. Sure enough, the other dog kissed her right back. All of this was too cute for words, but I sensed that something much deeper was unfolding before us. Our beast from the streets was gaining some degree of self-awareness, some new consciousness about herself and how to relate to others. I don't know how else to put it, and I had no idea what it might have meant, but I knew that something important was taking hold.

What I can say with certainty, though, is that after Zelda's mirror, mirror episode, we made the breakthrough. One morning, with another handful of treats, I said to Zelda, "Sit!"—and sit she did. Certain this was only a fluke, never again to be repeated. I again said "Sit!" and down she sat. Again and again she repeated the feat, and I was elated. I felt like Henry Higgins had with Eliza Doolittle, when she finally mastered "The rain in Spain . . ." I could even hear the song from *My Fair Lady* ringing in my ears. Now Zelda became a breeze to teach. She learned "Speak!" "Lie down!" "Roll over!" and "Give me your paw!" Every command she happily obeyed—even when I stopped rewarding her with treats. Eda and I were thrilled and relieved, of course, and Sheela went rushing over to the butcher for a fresh load of spare ribs. Party time! Our little girl was on her way.

That spring, Indira Gandhi got a little training, too. Like many charismatic leaders who muzzle the press and surround themselves with sycophants, she had somehow managed to convince herself that she could suspend civil liberties, jail her opponents, and systematically govern against the will of her people—and still be reelected to another term as prime minister. On Election Day, though, hundreds of millions of people across India—rich and poor, and from every caste and tribe—stood for hours in the heat and dust to express their feelings with the only tool they had at hand: their vote. And with one majestic stroke of the peoples' pen, Indira Gandhi was summarily and peacefully removed from power.

For Myron and me, this was very moving to see and report. For two years, Mrs. Gandhi and her entourage had argued that democracy was a luxury that India simply could not afford. India, they said, was too vast and diverse, its problems were too complex, its people too primitive and uninformed. Moreover, freedom and democracy, they argued, were not native to India. They were unwanted vestiges of colonial rule; India had to cast them off and find its own form of government, its own solutions to its economic and social problems. Many respected Indian journalists and intellectuals shared those views, and many of them were absolutely stunned when Mrs. Gandhi was shunted out of office. The morning after the election, the opposition Janata Party and its supporters paraded through the streets of New Delhi in trucks and buses, with horns honking and music blaring. It was like a national holiday. Sanjoy Hazarika, an Indian journalist, stood with me watching the parade. "Paul, do you know what happened?" he said. "We all underestimated the wisdom of our people."

One Sunday afternoon in the midst of this upheaval, Eda and I were having lunch with our pals John and Chris Needham. We were out on our porch when suddenly Eda leaned in and whispered to me, "Can I see you for a minute, in private?"

"Excuse us," I said to John and Chris. "We'll be right back."

"Guess what," Eda said.

"You mean . . .?"

"Yes. I think my water just broke."

We made our apologies to Chris and John, packed a bag for Eda, and rushed off to Duke Chawla's East-West Clinic. The labor was far from easy—it took over twelve hours—but at five o'clock the next morning, Eda gave birth to a handsome baby boy, whom we later named Justin. The baby arrived breach, as we had feared, but Eda's confidence proved wholly justified: Her doctor delivered the baby without a hitch.

After the long night in labor, Eda and I were thrilled and exhausted, and once mother and child were peacefully asleep, I walked out of the clinic to look for a taxi and go home to collapse. I did not have far to look.

Outside, sleeping behind the wheel of his taxi, was Punjab Singh. He had rushed us to the clinic the night before, and though I had paid him and told him to go home, Punjab had stayed the whole night through, waiting, worrying, eager to be sure that all of us came through okay. In my eyes, the man was an absolute prince.

I slid into the front seat beside him and as we headed back to Jor Bagh I gave Punjab a full report. He put his hand on my shoulder, but he was too choked up to talk. For a long time he drove without saying a word, and I could see that he was trying to fully absorb the enormity of the moment. "You are a very lucky man, Sahib," he finally said. "You come to India alone, you meet a wonderful woman, and now she brings you a son. A son! What wonderful feelings this must be bringing to you . . ."

With that, I abruptly burst into tears. During the night, my world, my consciousness, had permanently shifted. Science and reason can explain many things, but they cannot fully explain the wonder of birth and life, and they cannot even begin to describe the delicacy of a baby's finger or the smell of skin that has come fresh from the womb. Holding that tiny being in my hands, feeling the life pulsing inside him, something had burst open inside me, I had felt a flood of emotion, an emotion more powerful and more beautiful than anything I had ever felt or could even imagine. Justin was born and, in some inexplicable way, so was I.

Punjab respectfully waited until I regained my composure, then he said to me, "Sahib, I can tell you one thing: This is the most important day of your life. From today everything changes, and nothing in your life will ever be the same. Nothing will ever be more important to you than that boy and the ones that will follow. That is just the way it is written, and that is the way it always will be."

Punjab was exactly right. A few days later, I brought Eda and baby Justin home and everything had changed. Eda had gone from Wonder Woman to Wonder Mother; every cell in her being was now attuned to our baby's every need and desire. He asked; she fulfilled. No words were necessary. It was the same with Sheela: She went from cook to grandma in the blink of an eye. When Eda needed a break, Sheela bathed the baby, powdered him, cradled him, sang to him; and if he was crying and unable to sleep, Sheela, drawing on some ancient maternal wisdom, would give him an expert, loving massage, and the baby would magically settle down and drift off to sleep. I was in awe of both of them. Watching Sheela, watching Eda with the baby at her breast, I thought: This is it, Mother and Child. The Power of Woman. We men may have our virtues, but women are connected to primal forces that are simply beyond our reach.

Zelda also underwent a profound transformation. In the evenings, Zelda and I would still go out to the park to play ball, and at the end of our session the unruly little beast would still run around me in circles, and she would still leap up and bite me on the bottom. But from the second we brought the baby home, Zelda never jumped up on our bed again. When the baby was being fed or changed, Zelda would always stand a respectful distance away, watching, guarding, a sentinel on alert. And when Eda brought the baby outside for some fresh air and a nap in the shade, Zelda would lay down quietly beside his basket, to watch over him and protect him from the crows.

CHAPTER FIVE

The Invisible Cord

Zelda had mysterious quirks and powers.

One evening during the height of The Emergency, our local postman in Jor Bagh rode up to our gate on his bicycle, and Zelda greeted him with a low, angry growl. This was very strange. Zelda knew our postman well; he came by every morning and Zelda had never before raised a word of fuss. Was it just the unusual hour of his appearance that set her on edge? At first I thought so. But then the postman handed me a special-delivery letter, and it had an ominous look. It was marked "Government of India," and it was closed with an official red wax seal.

The letter inside was chilling. It was from the "Office of the Chief Censor," and it contained an official warning: "Mr. Chutkow, it has been noted that you have failed to provide the Censor's Office with copies of all of the dispatches that you have written for the Associated Press. This is a clear and flagrant violation of India's censorship guidelines. Any further failure in this regard will result in your immediate expulsion from the territory of India. Sincerely yours . . ." I read the warning twice, and then I looked down at Zelda and thought, "Could she possibly have sensed . . .?"

Instantly, I swatted the idea away: "Come on, man. Cut the mush!" But then other things happened, and they all made me wonder.

One morning, for instance, Eda and I took Zelda out for a leisurely walk to our local market in Jor Bagh. Apart from tugging on the leash a bit, Zelda was very well behaved—until we came to the Pig Po, our neighborhood butcher. Twenty paces from their door, Zelda pulled in her tail, stiffened her legs, and refused to move. I prodded, I cajoled, and finally I commanded, but Zelda simply would not budge. Then I walked in front of her and tried to drag her past the Pig Po, but she planted all four paws into the ground and pulled back on the leash with all her might. Finally we had to retreat ten yards, then circle around the butcher shop a safe distance away. What was this all about? The smell of the meat? A fear of winding up butchered inside? Had someone at the Pig Po once whacked her with a broom? Eda and I had no answers.

And then there were the nightmares. Zelda would be sleeping soundly on the living room couch or on her bed and suddenly she would start whining and wailing in her sleep. Then she'd start shaking, head to tail. The poor girl was in torment. When these attacks came on, I would stroke her back and lightly scratch her ears, but nothing helped until the dream subsided. All my life I'd had dogs, but never one who suffered agonizing dreams the way Zelda did. What stirred this beast? What strange forces roiled inside her?

Then one day Eda and Sheela noticed something else that was a little strange: Sheela would fill her bowl around 7 p.m., but Zelda would not eat her dinner until I got home. Sometimes on a heavy news day, Myron and I would not finish filing our stories until late, and I might not get home till midnight or even later. No matter: Zelda would not touch her food until she had greeted me at the door and assured herself that I was okay. At first Eda and I dismissed this as just another of Zelda's bizarre little quirks, but Sheela saw this in a very different light. "Indian wife," Sheela explained. "Never eat till husband home."

Indian wife? The dog?

All I could do was shake my head in wonder. What a strange little beast she was, and in many ways she seemed the perfect distillation of India itself: wild and exotic, always enchanting, often vexing, and perpetually moved by raw subterranean forces that defied all logic and reason, forces that constantly led us into realms that stretched far beyond the rims of our imagination.

There was, for instance, the time I traveled to the River Ganges, India's holy river, for the opening of the Kumbh Mela, the most sacred of Hindu pilgrimages. Long before dawn, I rode through the streets of Allahabad in the back of a bicycle rickshaw; all was quiet and still except for the grunts of my driver and the rhythmic whir of his tires against the pavement. But then we turned onto a long dirt road leading down to the river, and it was like entering a whole other world. Hundreds of brightly colored buses— from across India and far beyond—were parked helter-skelter along the road, each bus filled to overflowing with men, women, and children, pilgrims come to bathe in the holy water, needy souls in search of cleansing, healing, and spiritual renewal.

On this sacred day in this sacred spot, four million to five million Hindu pilgrims would come to the holy river, and when I arrived at the water's edge, a million or more were already there, spread along the banks as far as the eye could see. As I walked along, taking notes and taking pictures, I saw throngs of holy men in saffron robes, chanting and bobbing; I saw groups of sadhus, the most devout, naked and covered in ash; and out on the water I saw waves and waves of pilgrims arriving in small boats, some powered by sail, some by oar, and many of them lighting their way with tiny fires that burned in metal pans wedged into the bow. All around me, Hindu pilgrims were wading out into the river, the men in their T-shirts and underwear, the women in saris or shifts, many holding small silver bowls that glinted dimly through the early morning mist. The men and boys swam far out and immersed themselves, while the women and girls stayed in close to shore and used the bowls to pour the holy water over their heads and necks and down their arms to the tips of their fingers, the way their ancestors had done for thousands of years.

Hindu philosophers speak of karma and the wheel of life; there, beside the Ganges, the wheel of life seemed to be rolling in front of my eyes. Right on shore, babies were being born—for a Hindu family, nothing could be more auspicious—and out on the water I watched the oldest and frailest among the pilgrims wade out the farthest and linger the longest, hoping, praying that the hand of death would come out to greet them, here in this holiest of places and with the sweetest of blessings. This was Hindu India down in its marrow, this was life and death in their naked truth, this was spiritual fervor and intensity on a scale that I could not even begin to fathom.

And then there was Mother Teresa.

One morning during a slow news period in New Delhi, I took an Indian Airlines flight to Calcutta, now known as Kolkata, and went to see Mother Teresa. My intention was purely journalistic: Indira Gandhi was a giant in her realm of Indian life; Mother Teresa was a giant in hers. To properly cover India for the world, via the AP's global network, I felt I had to meet her face-to-face and see her storied work among the poorest of the poor.

At the airport in Calcutta, I found a taxi and gave the driver my intended address. "Ah, Mother," he said with a knowing smile. "You have come to meet her. This is good. Very, very good."

The headquarters of Mother Teresa's Missionaries of Charity was located in a ramshackle neighborhood on the edge of the city, and when I arrived, a huge crowd was gathered outside. This, my driver explained, was a daily event: Mother provided a hot meal for anyone in need. I stepped from the taxi and was immediately swept into a disturbing sea: throngs of children, sad-eyed and emaciated, women in rags, old men on crutches, people missing limbs, blind people, sick people, dying people—it was like a group portrait of human suffering and pain. Milling around too were packs of wild, scavenging street dogs, each as hungry and desperate as our little Zelda had been. India is home to the Taj Mahal and other glories, but this too is India: life in the raw, life stripped naked, a feverish land where all of the majesty and all of the misery come straight in your face.

Inside Mother Teresa's door I found respite and calm. Everything inside was bright, cheerful, and immaculately clean. Scores of young, fresh-faced sisters were scurrying about, carrying trays, pushing food carts, all of them getting ready to feed their flock. In their crisp white habits with the distinctive blue stripes on the border, the sisters moved with brisk efficiency and a palpable sense of meaning and purpose. One of them led me in to Mother Teresa. She was working at her desk but she jumped up to greet me. "Thank you so much for coming!" she said, as if I were a long-lost friend. I put my hands together and bowed to her, Indian-style, and she did the same in return. Then she said, "You have had a very long journey, Paul. May I offer you a cup of tea?"

"Maybe later," I said.

"Good! We have so much to show you . . ."

I was instantly enthralled. Physically, Mother Teresa was a mere whisper of a woman, not even close to five feet tall, but her presence was so huge it filled the room. Her face radiated strength and character. She had big, even teeth, a thick peasant nose, eyes that were sunk back deep in their sockets, and the skin on her face was as tough and weathered as an old leather boot. She had been born in Yugoslavia, her mother and father had come from the rugged terrain of Albania, and she had been doing missionary work in the streets of Calcutta since the age of eighteen. All of the hardships and all of the cruelties she had lived and witnessed were now etched in her face, but her eyes showed nothing but wisdom and joy.

"Mother," as everyone called her, gave me a tour of her compound, and along the way she shared with me her values and her special point of view. "I feel so sorry for rich people," she told me. "All their money keeps them poor." In her eyes, most rich people were totally detached from the true beauty of life and its deeper meanings. For her, it is the poor who are the richest people on the face of this earth, for the poor are connected, deeply, to what is most sacred and most important. "The poor give us so much more than we give them," she said. "They're such strong people, living day to day with no food, and they never curse, never complain. We don't have to give them pity or sympathy; we have to learn from them."

When the sisters began serving lunch to the people outside, Mother moved among them, greeting each person as an honored guest, bowing to them, smiling, clasping their hands in hers or just touching a shoulder or a hollow cheek. With those she knew best, Mother would joke and share with them her whimsical little chuckle. "What wonderful work you do," I said to her. She just laughed and brushed that aside: "This is not my work, Paul. It's His."

Mother Teresa started the order of the Missionaries of Charity in 1950, and from the outset, to maintain total independence, she made it her policy to accept no financial assistance from the Indian government, only the occasional gift of land for new projects she had developed in various Indian cities. The only money she had for her missions in India and other developing countries was what she could raise from private donors, and often it arrived in contributions of only a few dollars or rupees. Mother insisted that almost every dime or rupee go to help the poor, the sick, and the dying, and never into salaries or comfortable living quarters for herself or the sisters.

That afternoon the sisters served hundreds of meals—an Indian flatbread, a helping of dal, and a cup of hot soup—and I wondered how Mother's Missionaries of Charity could afford to do this every day, not just here but in their other missions throughout the developing world. Mother just smiled. "God is our banker. He always provides," she told me. "Here we feed about seven hundred people a day and we've never run out of food, not even once. One day we had nothing left, not a single piece of bread to give our people. And do you know what happened? For some mysterious reason, the schools were suddenly closed that day and their bread was sent over to us. Now tell me, Paul: Who else could have done that?"

Mother sensed that I remained a little skeptical, so she told me another story. "One year, just before Christmas, one of the young sisters came to me and asked for some money to buy ice cream for everyone. I told her it would be much too expensive. A day later someone sent in some money with a note saying to use it for ice cream. See? That's the delicate love of God. So beautiful, isn't it?"

Beautiful it was. From there, following Mother Teresa's plan for me, I spent three days inside her mission, watching and listening. I visited health clinics and sat in on birth-control classes for teenage girls, cooking and nutrition classes for young mothers, and reading and math classes for the hundreds of abandoned children now living under Mother's care. At the end of my last day, one of the sisters led me into the room where they housed and cared for men and women with leprosy. The lepers.

Leprosy is an affliction with a history tracing back four thousand years, and it has always been shrouded in superstition, ignorance, and fear. Across Asia and Africa, lepers are frequently shunned, stigmatized, and put into camps and colonies to isolate their contagion, and those afflicted have often been treated with violence and derision. Not here. At Mother Teresa's, the leper ward looked and felt like a small cathedral. The walls were freshly painted and they rose up to a very high ceiling. At the very top was a ribbon of windows, and when I arrived, the late afternoon sun was streaming in, sending a soft purple light down onto the beds below.

The beds were set in two parallel rows, with a broad walkway down the middle, and I could see that each bed was spotless and freshly made, giving the entire room a feeling of great dignity and pride. This was the men's ward—the women were cared for across the hall—and on each bed sat a man with lesions on his face or arm, or on his hands or feet. Four young nuns moved from bed to bed, offering water and fluffing pillows, or bathing the men and cleansing their wounds. As they worked, the nuns chatted with the men, touching them, joking with them, brightening their lives. I wish I could capture in words the look I saw on those sisters' faces. To me, these young women looked absolutely radiant and totally at peace, as if there were nothing else on this earth they would rather be doing.

It was Mother, I knew, who had shown them the way. "I see God in every human being," she once said. "When I wash that leper's wounds, I feel I am nursing the Lord himself. Is it not a beautiful experience?"

At the end of my three-day immersion in her spirit and work, Mother Teresa invited me into her private study for a cookie and a hot cup of tea. For a long time we sat together in comfortable silence; she knew how profoundly I had been moved. Then she said to me softly, "Come up with me and see Jesus."

I followed her upstairs and into a large, airy room that was totally empty, except for the crucifix mounted on the wall. Mother Teresa knelt down on the cool linoleum, facing Jesus, and she motioned me to kneel down beside her. In a quiet, intimate voice, she said a prayer in Latin, and then her voice grew softer and she began to lay down her burdens. She told Jesus about her day, about the young sister who had arrived that morning, about her meeting that afternoon with a city official who was helping her build a new clinic close by. Mother chatted with Jesus as if they were best friends and partners, resuming a conversation they had started early that morning. I couldn't hear Him, but I felt certain that Jesus was responding to her with words of comfort and support. He was her pillar, her rock, her constant source of strength and inspiration.

When she had finished, I stood up, deeply shaken and a little disoriented. Seeing my face, Mother chuckled and took me by the arm. I think she somehow knew exactly what I was thinking: What's a nice Jewish boy doing in a place like this?

When I was leaving, I hugged Mother and told her that I hoped to see her again one day. "Oh, you will, Paul," she laughed. "You definitely will!"

When I got back to the AP bureau in New Delhi, I wrote a nice story about Mother Teresa and her work, but the best parts I kept for myself. Later I shared some of it with Eda, but not very much. It was too raw to talk about yet, and I knew it might take a long time for it all to sink in, for all of it to tie together, if it ever could.

Then late one night, after Eda had fed Justin and fallen asleep beside him, I was sitting out on the front porch with my pal Zelda, watching the moonlight dance on the leaves of the big flame tree standing in the darkness across the way. In Mother's world, I now could see, there were no boundaries of nationality or creed, there were no differences of color or caste, there were no labels, no limits, no questions to answer. In her eyes, the truth was simple and plain to see: Young or old, weak or strong, blind or leper, king or beggar, we were all in this together; we were all bound to one another by one powerful, invisible cord, a cord held by an invisible hand, a hand leading all of us forward with a meaning and purpose that we may never be lucky enough or wise enough to see or apprehend.

Seeing the world through Mother's eyes, everything now made sense to me. Living in New York, a divorced and solitary man, I had never dreamed of coming to India, not even once. But here I was, just two years later, wildly in love, a husband, a father, and bound by that invisible cord to a whole family of enchanting characters: Eda. Justin. Sheela. Myron. Punjab Singh. Dhobi Dubinsky. And now I knew we were forever bound to Zelda, too. Out of all the millions of doors in India, this little dog had somehow managed to find her way to ours, and now she nips me playfully on the bottom and watches over Justin with all the love and devotion of a guardian angel.

Now, as I looked out into the night, I could almost hear Mother chuckle.

CHAPTER SIX

A Moveable Feast

Sheela's love for Zelda knew no bounds.

In the morning, she would give Zelda warm milk and a generous helping of meat, rice, and vegetables, cooked together into an enticing stew. During the day she gave Zelda little treats in the kitchen, maybe a rib bone or a warm chapati, and at night, after she helped Eda put the baby to bed, Sheela and Zelda would often sit down together and have a love-in. Sheela would scratch Zelda up and down her tummy and behind her ears, and Zelda would nuzzle in with tenderness and affection. If Sheela stopped, Zelda would pull at her hand with her paw until she got more. "Luckiest dog in India," Sheela always said, and watching them together, I knew that Sheela felt mighty lucky, too. We all did.

But I knew it had to end.

The international news business feeds on crisis and conflict, not on the tempered workings of democratic governance. After Mrs. Gandhi and her party were ousted from power, the new government quickly restored democratic freedoms, released political prisoners, and removed the rules and regulations that for two years had muzzled the lively Indian press. It was beautiful to watch: The world's largest democracy was regaining its bearings. Once the crisis had subsided, though, India as a story quickly slipped from the front pages of the world, and I knew that an exodus of foreign correspondents was sure to follow.

Myron was the first to leave. A few months after Mrs. Gandhi's defeat, Myron got the word: The AP named him bureau chief in London, with responsibility for the whole of the United Kingdom and key parts of Africa and the Middle East. This was one of the plum jobs in the AP and in all of American journalism. It was a tribute to Myron's many talents and his decade of distinguished reporting across the Asian subcontinent. I was thrilled for Myron and his family, but for the press corps in New Delhi, both foreign and domestic, this marked the end of an era, and for me it marked the end of an illuminating apprenticeship at the side of a master.

Myron was more than a superb correspondent. As I saw over the two years we worked together, he was also a diplomat of amazing skill and grace. As president of the South Asian Foreign Correspondents Association, Myron played a crucial role during Mrs. Gandhi's National Emergency. He was our emissary to the Indian government, our go-between with the Chief Censor's Office, and as a man who had devoted eleven years of his life to India—with Rachel, his Indian wife, and their two children, Yael and Josh—Myron stood as a one-man rebuke to Mrs. Gandhi's constant refrain that the foreign press corps was a bunch of spies and enemies of the state, out to destabilize India and damage its future. Mrs. Gandhi's assertions made headlines around the world, but among the journalists and opinion-makers in New Delhi and beyond, such claims served only to damage her credibility and darken her legacy. In the eyes of many, Myron's calm, factual dispatches carried far more weight than all of her government's self-serving pronouncements and decrees.

In the months that followed, the exodus accelerated. Bill Borders would soon leave: *The New York Times* rewarded his work in India with a prized post in its London bureau. Sharon Rosenhause, the gifted and sardonic correspondent of *The Los*

Angeles Times—and a favorite tennis and Scrabble partner of ours—landed a big job with the paper back in LA, and several members of the Reuters crew were moving on as well. For Eda and me, this was the close of a very special time: The crisis in India had brought us all together and now we felt like we were losing a whole family of friends, people who had shared in our wedding, the birth of Justin, Sheela's artistry in the kitchen, and, of course, our crazy adventures with Zelda.

And then our turn came: Paris.

Part of me was elated at the news—Paris was the assignment I had trained for and longed for ever since I joined the AP. But another part of me was thrown into turmoil: What would happen to Sheela and Zelda? They were family now; how could we ever leave them behind? Eda and I were riddled with questions. Would Sheela want to leave India and come with us to Paris, if somehow we could arrange it? And what about Zelda? Would the French government even let the little monster in?

Sheela's situation was very complex. She had been born into a dirt-poor family in Kanpur, southeast of New Delhi, and as a young girl she had been sent off to be a servant with a British family. It could have been a horrible experience, but the family took her in as one of their own, and she had remained in close touch with them even after they moved back to Britain. By the time I arrived in India, Sheela had a good job working as the cook for Jacques Leslie, the *LA Times* man in New Delhi at the start of The Emergency. Alas, when one of Jacques's stories piqued the ire of Mrs. Gandhi and her censors, Jacques was summarily expelled from India and Sheela was out of a job—for about five minutes. Eda and I instantly grabbed her, and right away she became an essential part of our family. But now what? As soon as we heard about the Paris assignment, Eda and I very gingerly told Sheela the news. "I'm very happy for you," Sheela said with her usual graciousness, but we could see the worry in her eyes. "Don't worry, Sheela," I said. "You're in God's pocket. Everything will work out okay."

I said the words, but frankly I had my doubts. Sheela had no birth certificate, no passport, no knowledge of French, and I saw no way we could bring her to Paris and support her for the rest of her life. Not on an AP salary. At the same time, we knew she could find a good job in New Delhi; for starters, many of our friends would be standing in line to hire her. So Eda and I were left in a terrible dilemma. How could we possibly take Sheela along? But how could we possibly leave her behind?

We faced a similar dilemma with Zelda. Could we really take her to Paris? We'd probably be in an apartment there; how would Zelda adapt to being cooped up inside? And might there be some sort of quarantine, as there was for dogs being brought into Britain? I checked with Michael Garin, the bureau chief for Agence France Press, and he felt sure there would be no such restriction, but for help he suggested I go right to the top: to the French ambassador to India. The ambassador? For a lowly dog? Well, it was for Zelda, after all, so I put in the call.

I expected the ambassador's reaction to be sniffy: What? You want to take a common Indian pi dog to Paris, the City of Light? *Mon Dieu*. But I was entirely wrong. The ambassador, it turned out, was a dog lover himself, and he found the idea utterly charming. In fact, he said that if I produced an official certificate showing that Zelda had received the proper rabies and other shots, he would give me a personal note for French customs officials. Sweet, I thought. I'll go back to Dr. Karb, get the certificate, and our little Zelda will be on her way. Her magical odyssey from the gutters of India would soon land her in the salons and bistros of Paris. How perfect this would be!

Alas, it was not as simple as that.

The next day I went back to the presidential stables and found Dr. Karb, and while he was happy to help with the necessary papers for Zelda, he also delivered me a very stern warning. "Mr. Chutkow, I can see that this little girl still has you in thrall, but I must be extremely honest with you: The trip will probably kill her."

"What?"

"Yes, Mr. Chutkow, I have seen it happen over and over. The flight to Paris is very long, isn't it? Fifteen hours or more, is it not so?"

"Well, yes . . ."

"And she will be in a very small cage, am I correct?"

"Well, yes . . ."

"That will put a terrible strain on her body. The dehydration alone could kill her. And there are so many unknowns. Some airlines have cargo areas where they do a proper job of controlling the temperature and air pressure, but many do not. And what happens if there is a mechanical mishap and the plane sits on the ground for a long time, in our blazing Indian heat? What then, Mr. Chutkow? The poor dog will suffer terribly."

"I see . . ."

"You go think it over, Mr. Chutkow. Then I know that you will do the right thing. At least I hope so."

This was sobering, to say the least. The road to hell, my mother was fond of saying, is paved with good intentions. Maybe she was right in this case. And maybe Dr. Karb was right too: The risks were just too high. Maybe, I thought, we should just do our best to find Zelda a good home in New Delhi and leave it at that. Yes, maybe that was the thing to do.

In the midst of our tribulations about Sheela and Zelda, terrorists struck—not our front-yard crows this time, real terrorists with murder on their minds. A cell of the Japanese Red Army hijacked a Japan Air Lines 747, with 156 people aboard, and forced it to land in the Bangladesh capital, Dacca, now known as Dhaka. The terrorists threatened to execute the passengers unless the Japanese government forked over $6 million in ransom and released nine of their comrades being held in jail. As soon as we got the word, John Needham of UPI and I were both on the next plane to Dacca.

When we landed, we saw that the story was very complicated to cover. All of the action was unfolding right there at the airport, but this was before the era of laptops and cell phones and there was no way to file stories internationally from there at the scene. So while John went to find the local UPI stringer, I went into town and set up headquarters at the Sheraton Hotel, which I knew had good phone and telex services. Within the hour, I had two AP stringers at the airport, giving me updates whenever they could convince an airport official to lend them a phone. With that system in place, I composed and filed stories via the telex in the hotel, sending them to the AP bureau in London or AP headquarters in New York, whichever I could reach first.

This system was working fairly well—until early the next morning. Just before dawn, as I was writing an update, I heard a burst of machine-gun fire spatter against the front of the hotel. Some of the bullets hit right below my window. I peered out and saw a tank from the Bangladeshi army parked in the driveway below. What the heck was this? Did the Japanese terror cell have accomplices inside the hotel? No. With two phone calls, I got the gist of what was unfolding: With the top brass of the government and army gathered at the airport to cope with the JAL crisis, a group of rogue army officers had decided this was the perfect moment to launch a coup d'état. They had moved swiftly. While one group tried to seize control of the Sheraton, another group stormed the airport command center where the bigwigs were—and most of the press corps, too. *Sheee-it*, was my AP team in the line of fire? Was my pal John Needham in there, too? I had no way of knowing. About an hour later, though, John came bursting through my door, white as a ghost: "Give me a drink. Quick!"

Yes, John had been there. When the rogue officers stormed in, with machine guns blazing, a Reuters man pulled John to safety, bullets whistling past the both of them. Fortunately, regular army forces reacted quickly and quelled the uprising. John came away shaken, but not deeply stirred; a little whiskey and he was good as new. "So, Paulie," he said, "are you sure you want to go off to Paris and miss all this fun?"

"And you, Johnny boy? How can we ever top this—a hijacking and a coup d'état rolled into one!"

The hijacking ended with a capitulation by the Japanese government. The terrorists got their $6 million in ransom and the release of six of their nine jailed comrades. Japanese officials put the best possible face on their cave-in, proclaiming that saving innocent lives was their top priority, far more important than the money they paid. Maybe so. But John and I both knew this outcome would only embolden other terrorists around the globe. Soon, we in the media would again be their helpless accomplices, forced to give international exposure to whatever their demands and complaints would be the next time around. Media manipulation was an essential part of the terrorists' game—and there wasn't a damn thing we could do to stop it.

I spent several days in Dacca, covering the story through to the finish, and when I finally arrived back at our front gate, Eda and Sheela, with Justin in tow, rushed out to greet me. But not Zelda. She hung back and wouldn't come anywhere near me, not even when I got down on my hands and knees and begged her to come. What the heck was this about?

Sheela had the answer: "She afraid you not come back." Yes, I could see it was true: My little Indian "wife" was afraid I had gone off and left her—and would never return. *You crazy monster*, I thought. Then I grabbed a tennis ball and took her out to play. Soon all was forgiven, but now I knew we had no choice in the matter: We had to find a way to take Zelda to Paris. There was simply no way we could leave her behind.

A day or two later I began looking for the safest way to ship a dog to Paris. I called several of the airlines that flew from India to Europe, and all of them were very eager to have our business. And with good reason: For long relocations, the AP paid for first-class tickets—a welcome profit for the airline. Still, when I dug deeper into how various carriers handled dogs during the flight, I could see that Dr. Karb was right: Few of them sounded totally reliable in this domain, and a few even refused to ship a dog that far. Too risky. Then I went to see the head of Air France in New Delhi. Like the French ambassador, he was eager to help, and he insisted that Air France cargo areas and crews were superbly equipped to handle dogs on long-distance flights. We would fly first-class, he assured me, and so would our little Zelda. "You can count on us, Mr. Chutkow. We will get the little lady to Paris safe and sound. I am giving you my word of honor."

"Little lady?" I couldn't help but smile.

There were still risks, of course, but Eda and I were now of one mind: Zelda was going to Paris, via Air France, no less. Then we worked out the plan. Zelda would "vacation" with the Needhams until we found a place to live in Paris, then Chris and John would escort her to the airport in plenty of time to get her through customs and onto the Air France flight. Animal lovers that they were, as well as devoted friends, John and Chris were happy to oblige. Then we found someone to build us a crate for Zelda's journey, and Dr. Karb supplied us with a sedative to keep Zelda calm throughout the flight. As promised, the French ambassador to India provided the requisite papers for the customs people in Paris. And so it was done: Our Zelda would soon be on her way to Paris.

Destiny, as it turned out, was smiling on Sheela, too. Or was it that invisible cord at work? Either way, in the midst of all this, Eda got a call from out of the blue. It was from Bim Bissell, a lovely, very capable Indian woman we knew in New Delhi. "Eda," she said, "I'm calling you for an unusual reason. I'm looking for a wonderful cook, someone very special. Might you, by chance, know of someone whom I might interview?"

Well, "by chance," Eda did know someone. But ever the careful lawyer, Eda was not about to disclose too much. "Who's this for, Bim?""

"Ken and Kitty Galbraith."

Oh my. "Ken" was none other than John Kenneth Galbraith, the esteemed economist, author, Harvard professor, and formerly President John F. Kennedy's ambassador to India. During the Galbraiths' tenure in India, Bim had served as Kitty's appointments secretary, and they had remained close ever since. The Galbraiths, Bim explained, were missing India terribly and were looking for a cook and housekeeper for their home in Cambridge, Massachusetts. Of course, the Galbraiths would pay all expenses to America and provide excellent living quarters and a good salary too, plus proper medical care and other necessities. Oh, and there was something else, Bim said. Every winter, the Galbraiths go to Gstaad, Switzerland, for a month or so. Their new cook would go to Europe with them, all expenses paid, of course. Right away Eda had visions of Sheela stopping off in Paris along the way. How perfect this could be!

"Well, Bim," Eda said, or words to this effect, "I just may have someone for you. I'll check with her and get back to you as soon as I can."

With Eda as go-between, Bim then met with Sheela and saw that she would be a perfect fit for the Galbraith family. And Sheela seemed very pleased as well, as if this were simply a part of some grand plan that she couldn't fathom but was quite content to accept. So then and there the deal was sealed: Sheela was going to America! Her future would be secure—and she would come see us in Paris on a regular basis. With cool efficiency, Eda then helped Sheela get everything she needed: a copy of her birth certificate, an Indian passport, and, with Bim smoothing the way, the necessary visa from the U.S. Embassy. Once everything was in order, the Galbraiths sent Sheela a ticket for Boston, with a short stopover in Paris to see us on the way. For Eda and me, this was almost too much to believe, but Sheela herself seemed totally unfazed by this dramatic turn in her life, as if she had known all along a miracle would happen. Well, I said to myself, I guess Sheela truly is in God's pocket.

At this stage, I was thrilled that Sheela and Zelda would still be important parts of our lives, but what about Punjab Singh and Dhobi Dubinsky? They, too, were like family now. One day, as we were packing up the house, Punjab drove up to our gate in his weather-beaten black and yellow taxi. I was surprised and immediately went out to see what was on his mind. I was planning to give him a gift as a thank you for his help and friendship, but I didn't have it ready yet. "Sahib," he said, "we are all very sorry to see you and Memsahib leave India. But you must please do me a very big favor, something very, very important to me."

"Of course, Punjab. Anything you want."

"It would be a great honor for me to take you and Memsahib and the baby to the airport. Just like when baby was born."

What a man. A mensch in a turban. I gave him a big hug and a squeeze. "Punjab," I said, "we would love nothing more."

A few days later, as we were having breakfast out on the porch, with Justin napping in his red baby chair, the dhobi rode up on his bicycle and gave us his usual sheepish bow. Then, visibly upset, he began jabbering in Hindi. Sheela arrived to translate. "He wants to go with you to America," Sheela said. Paris, America, it was all the same to Dhobi Dubinsky. "He says there must be lots and lots of laundry there."

"Wait right here," I said.

I went back to the bedroom, called the Jor Bagh taxi stand, and asked Punjab to please come by. Then I took out a special envelope that I had prepared for the dhobi. I had been saving it for this very moment.

When Punjab arrived, I ushered the dhobi into the backseat with me and asked Punjab to take us to the AP office downtown. On the way, I handed the dhobi the envelope. Inside was some money for him and a copy of a story I had written about him, a story that had been published in a big spread in *TheWashington Post*. The spread contained a poignant photo of the dhobi, in his little vest as always, holding his baby girl in his arms. When he saw it, Mr. Dubinsky could not believe his eyes.

The story recounted what had happened to the dhobi and his family during one of the nastiest moments of Mrs. Gandhi's National Emergency. In an effort to clean up the capital on the eve of a big international conference, a team of government goons had come to the shantytown where the dhobi and his wife and baby were living. With no warning and no protest permitted, the goons bulldozed the shacks and tossed all the belongings of the families onto the backs of government trucks. Then they loaded the men, women, and children into waiting buses. They drove the families to a huge, empty stretch of land about ten miles out of town and just dumped them there. Using string, someone had divided the land into tiny plots, about eight-foot square, and each family had been allotted one plot provided they had the money to build something on it. There was one bus a day that would ferry the men and women to and from their jobs back in the city. *Congratulations, folks,* was the message. *Thanks to the largesse of your government, you are now going to be homeowners!*

This was tyranny at work, brutal and arbitrary, and the dhobi had been one of its many helpless victims. During The Emergency, I hadn't dared give the dhobi a copy of *The Washington Post* story; I feared that if anyone saw it, he might face reprisals. Now, though, it seemed a safe thing to do. The dhobi could not read a single word on the page, but for a long time he ran the tips of his bony fingers over the face of his daughter, as if he could feel the softness of her skin right through the paper. Then he asked me something in Hindi, and Punjab translated:

"Sahib, he wants to know if he can keep the photo."

"Yes, of course. It's my gift to him."

The dhobi bowed and clasped his hands in front of him, and very carefully placed the clipping back in its envelope beside the money. Then he let forth with another torrent, the gist of which was, "Please, please, Sahib, take me to America; the streets are surely paved with laundry."

I couldn't do that, but I was determined to help. When we arrived at the AP office, I introduced Dhobi Dubinsky to Gene Kramer, Myron's successor as bureau chief. Gene had just found an apartment, and I insisted that he hire the dhobi to do his laundry. Gene agreed, albeit reluctantly, and they came to terms: The dhobi would start the following week. "If he loses a single sock, I'm going to fire him," Gene said.

"And if you do," I said, "I will personally fly back here and wring your neck!"

"It means that much to you?" Gene asked.

"Yes, that much and more."

On the morning of our departure, everything was ready to go. Our household belongings had been packed up and shipped to Paris. Zelda had a new, handcrafted wooden crate to travel in, complete with a water dish, her blanket, a few of her toys, and her sedatives in an envelope taped to the top. The Needhams had her papers, her Air France ticket, and a big pot of her dog food, specially prepared by Sheela, of course. As soon as we sent word, the Needhams would send our little Zellie on her way. For her part, Sheela was going to spend a few days with her son, Tony, and his family, then pack her bags and fly to Boston, stopping on the way to see us in Paris.

At nine o'clock that night, Punjab Singh pulled up to our gate at 108 Jor Bagh. He was wearing a freshly washed shirt and turban to mark the occasion. Eda got in the backseat with Justin in her arms, and I helped Punjab load his trunk with our suitcases, Eda's carry-on, my camera bag, a flight bag filled with baby needs, a fresh banana bread baked by Sheela, and heaven only knows what else. It was, in every sense, a moveable feast.

Before long, the three of us were aboard the big Air France 747, and as the plane lifted into the sky, we watched the lights of New Delhi recede in the distance. The top bubble of the 747 had been made into a lounge for the first-class passengers, and now it held a magnificent spread: champagne, huge trays of smoked salmon, foie gras, puff pastries, a half wheel of brie, several cuts of Camembert, and a lovely selection of red and white wines. After the other passengers went down to sleep, Eda, Justin, and I had the lounge to ourselves. While Justin played along the leather couches, Eda and I raised a toast to each other with glasses of very fine champagne.

Then I sank back and let the feelings rush over me. What a transformative experience India had been. Up close and very personal, I had witnessed tyranny and terror, misery and squalor, and right beside them I had seen strength and beauty, character and courage, wisdom and heavenly grace. How rich I felt. Twenty-six months before, I had arrived in India alone and with a single suitcase. Now I was leaving India with Eda and Justin beside me, Sheela would be joining us soon, and then would come our little Zelda, my Indian "wife" and closest pal.

Sheela was so right: Zelda certainly was "the luckiest dog in India." A year ago, she was infested with parasites, sleeping in filth, and eating garbage from gutters. Now, as I dozed off, I imagined Zelda on her own Air France flight to Paris, stretched out in the first-class cabin, eating foie gras and sipping the finest champagne.

Even Eliza Doolittle never had it this good.

Part Two:
Paris

CHAPTER SEVEN

Ah, Dog

Our first stop in Paris had to be the Tuileries Gardens

It was October and it was chilly—especially so after the heat of India—but on our very first morning in Paris, we bundled up, settled Justin into his stroller, and then we left our hotel and headed down the Champs-Élysées. It was a bit of a shock, going from the poverty of India to the opulence of Paris, but soon we were strolling through the Tuileries Gardens, under the chestnut trees, with marble sculptures by Aristide Maillol flanking us on either side. When we reached the big fountain in the middle, a dozen young boys were running around water chasing their sailboats, just as I had seen them doing ten years before.

This was the place; this was where my dream was born. Right here at this fountain. I was twenty years old at the time, and I was spending the summer in Paris and exploring the idea of becoming a writer. Elliott Coleman, the head of the Writing Seminars at Johns Hopkins University, was encouraging me in that direction, and Phoebe Stanton, my art history professor, was urging all her students to spend time in Paris and experience the art, the life, and the spirit. Paris, she told us, was not only a sensory and artistic feast; it was a place of exhilarating personal and intellectual freedom, a place to grow, a place to break free. I had to go. As it turned out, Will Furth, a childhood pal of mine, had landed a summer job with a French firm that made commercial displays, so we decided to go to Paris together. Being on tight student budgets, Will and I took rooms at a cheap hotel in the very north of the city, and from that base we explored Paris and made weekend excursions to Spain, Switzerland, and the south of France.

Mornings were for work. I would sit in my room or at our local cafe, writing sketches and stories, while Will went to his office in the bustling market area of Place du Marché St. Honoré, a short walk from the Tuileries Gardens. At lunchtime, I often kept right on working, but once or twice a week I'd take a break and go meet Will for lunch. Sometimes we went for a beer and a sandwich with his office mates, and sometimes we splurged and had a proper French lunch: three courses, from *pâte de campagne* on through to *crème caramel* or *mousse au chocolat.* From there Will and I would go to a *patisserie,* buy an éclair or an ice cream, and then we would install ourselves by the fountain in the Tuileries Gardens, to enjoy the sun and watch the parade of enticing young women sauntering by.

And what a glorious parade it was: The young French women so carefree in their tiny skirts and breezy summer blouses, exuding an allure and unfettered sexuality that we two lads from Chicago had never before encountered, much less tasted. The art we saw in Paris was fabulous, but this daily parade was even better. And so was watching those kids play with their sailboats around the fountain. Many of them would chase their boats with a running commentary in both French and English, switching effortlessly between the two, and then and there I thought, "Wow, this is it. This is the dream." Find the right woman, one rich in character and with an adventurous spirit, come here as a foreign cor-respondent, write about France and Europe, art and movies, food and wine, and together we'll raise adorable bilingual kids and have, quite simply, the time of our lives. Yes, that was the dream, and now, exactly ten years and three months later, here we were, Eda, Justin, and I, eating ice cream beside that same fountain in the Tuileries Gardens. It had taken me ten years of hard work, including four years of working graveyard shifts from midnight to 8 a.m., but at last we had arrived: Paris was ours. The dream was finally coming true.

Could it last? We could only hope and do our best.

Sheela arrived the following Saturday. While Eda stayed with Justin at the hotel, I took a taxi to the airport to pick her up. And when she emerged from customs, my jaw dropped to the floor: Sheela looked like a different woman. Gone were her sari and her open-toed sandals. Sheela was now dressed in stylish slacks and a colorful blouse, with a warm sweater wrapped around her, and she wore winter boots trimmed in fur. It was as if she had left her Indian self totally behind and was now ready for a whole new life in America. To my added surprise, Sheela came through customs carrying only a tiny shoulder bag. We hugged and fussed over each other, and then I said, "Sheela, where are the rest of your bags?"

"Oh, I checked them through to Boston," she said non-chalantly. "I'll pick them up when I get there."

Yes, that was our Sheela: Yesterday she had no passport and had never set foot on a plane; today she was a sophisticated world traveler, hopping effortlessly from continent to continent, yesterday New Delhi, tomorrow Boston, next week Gstaad. *This woman is amazing*, I thought. She'll have no trouble in America or with the Galbraiths—in no time flat she'll be the toast of Harvard and the whole Kennedy clan. Yup, there was no doubt about it: Our beloved Sheela was well on her way.

Zelda's arrival in Paris was not so graceful.

With a stroke of good fortune, Eda and I found a lovely apartment on the Left Bank, on the rue du Val de Grâce, near the southern tip of the Luxembourg Gardens. We wouldn't be able to move in for a few more days, but we immediately sent word to the Needhams: *Go!* Put Zelda on the next plane to Paris. Then one day I ran into Jean-Claude Suares, a friend of mine from New York who was vacationing in Paris. At the time, J.C., as everyone called him, was the art director of the Op-Ed page of *The New York Times*; we had met through David Schneiderman, a Hopkins pal of mine who was then the assistant editor of the Op-Ed page. J.C. was an absolute genius at illustration, and he had a gift for drawing animals and bringing out their hidden humor and spirit. As we chatted, J.C. said to me, "Let's have lunch on Saturday."

"Sorry, buddy, I can't," I said. "I've got to go to the airport."

"The airport? What for?"

"To pick up our dog."

"A dog? What kind of dog?"

"An Indian dog. A little mutt we rescued from the streets."

"I want to come," J.C. said.

J.C. loved animals, the more exotic the better, and I could see that his always vivid imagination was already running amok. "J.C., she's just a mutt," I said. "An ordinary mongrel."

"Shut up," he said. "I'm coming!"

So that Saturday morning, J.C. and I hopped into a taxi and headed for Charles de Gaulle Airport. Zelda's plane was due in at 10 a.m. On the way, I became increasingly nervous. I had total confidence in Air France, but it was still an awfully long flight. Would our little girl arrive okay? I had another worry, too. Our taxi driver, like many of the taxi drivers in Paris, was behind the wheel of an elegant Mercedes-Benz— I felt planets away from Punjab Singh—and sitting primly beside him was his dog, a miniature French poodle. The poodle was a bit smaller than Zelda, and there the resemblance abruptly stopped. This French poodle was a mass of steel-gray curls, freshly washed and blown dry, and she had a billow of carefully sculpted curls on the top of her head, fastened with a little red bow. She had on a jeweled leather collar, and her nails looked as though they had been trimmed and buffed at a very expensive Parisian salon. To make matters worse, the poodle was impeccably mannered. Sitting on her leather seat in the Mercedes, she held herself absolutely still, with her paws daintily forward, watching the riffraff out on the street with a quiet, almost regal air. Oh boy, I thought. If this is what Parisians view as the ideal dog, then we and Zelda are in for a world of hurt.

At Charles de Gaulle, J.C. and I were sent along to a customs area reserved for clearing cargo, and there, off in a corner, stood Zelda's crate. My heart immediately sank. Two of the front bars, made of thick wooden slats, were chewed through, and from thirty paces away I could see they were stained with blood. Zelda obviously had gone berserk and had tried to gnaw her way to freedom. So much for Dr. Karb's sedatives. But was she even alive? My worst fears now climbed up into my throat.

When we reached the crate, there stood Zelda, wild-eyed and still clawing to get out. I opened the door and she leapt into my arms, kissing me, hugging me, and then she jumped down and began to spin and spin and cry for what I assumed was joy. Then suddenly she stopped, planted her paws, and took a massive, inelegant dump. Right beside the customs desk. I was elated she was alive—and embarrassed beyond belief. Yes, our little Zelda had arrived in Paris, in all her raging glory.

"*Ç'est rien, Monsieur,*" the customs official said, with wonderful humor and forbearance. "*La petite a eu un très longue voyage!*" It's nothing, Monsieur. The little girl had a very long trip!

I corralled Zelda, put her on the leash, and found some paper towels and a plastic bag to clean up the mess. J.C.

watched all this in shock and disbelief. "This?" he finally said, his jaw quivering. "This is the dog you rescued and brought all the way from India? This?"

J.C. was crushed. He had obviously imagined some fabulous, exotic beast, maybe wearing a turban and with a diamond in her nose. Zelda did not quite live up to those expectations.

We breezed through the customs process—the letter from the French ambassador did the trick—and then we went for a walk outside to let Zelda stretch her legs and empty her bladder. Apart from the chewed front bars, the inside of her crate was pristine; the little girl had held it all the way, some fifteen hours or more. When she was done, we found a suitable taxi, a station wagon, and put Zelda in the back with us and her crate in the rear; I figured it was worth saving, if for nothing more than a conversation piece.

On the ride into Paris I was expecting the worst, but Zelda was the absolute picture of good manners. She snuggled into me for a while, then into J.C., and I was extremely proud of her; she had come a long, long way from the wild beast that used to rumple up our bed and bite me on the bottom. I told some of those stories to J.C. on the way into town, and he kept looking at her, puzzled, trying to take her all in.

When we reached our hotel, Zelda had a joyous reunion with Eda and Justin (Sheela by now had left for Boston) and then we fed Zelda and decided to go to lunch. We chose the Pizza Berri, a friendly place near our hotel and right across the street from the Paris bureau of the Associated Press, then located in the same building as *The International Herald Tribune*. Now came the great question: Do we take Zelda along with us to lunch or bribe the hotel concierge to watch her for an hour or so? Paris restaurants, we had been assured, were very welcoming to dogs—more so than to small children—but the question remained: How would they take to an uncouth beast like Zelda? Well, we threw caution to the wind and decided to find out. J.C., of course, came along with us; this was a show he was not about to miss.

The waiters at the Pizza Berri were marvelous. They found us a spacious booth in the back, where Justin could spread out between Eda and me, and under the table there was plenty of room for Zelda to spread out, too. We had a fine lunch—two big pizzas, salads, and crème caramel and we had some pizza left over. The waiters brought us a pizza box so we could take the rest with us, and right away J.C. went to work on the top of the box. By this time he had a vivid image swirling in his head, and that image now flowed merrily down his arm and out the tip of his pen. It was a wildly funny dog, exuding charm, and she was standing on her hind legs, head back, ready to down a huge slice of pizza that she held in her paw. He got her. In a sketch that took all of thirty seconds to create, J.C. nailed her, zany spirit and all. Now our Zellie really had arrived. Before long, I figured, her portrait would be hanging in the Louvre, just down the hall from the Mona Lisa. Welcome to Paris. Could life get any better than this?

And then it happened.

One night around 8:30 p.m., a week or so later, I was in the AP bureau, sending out a few soccer scores and preparing to shut down the American Desk. The French Desk was staffed around the clock; the rest of us were on call throughout the night, should any major news erupt. As I finished up, the phone rang: It was Eda, and she had a touch of panic in her voice. As she quickly explained, Justin was howling and in obvious pain. But she had no idea what was causing it. We had to get him to a doctor—right away. But what doctor? We had just arrived and we didn't know any.

Through an AP colleague, though, we got the name of a reputable pediatrician and within the hour we were in his examination room, with Justin howling even worse than before. The poor little guy was literally contorted in pain. The doctor did a careful examination, but he could not pinpoint the cause either. Earlier in the day, Justin had fallen against the side of his crib, and from that the doctor surmised that Justin, who was all of six months old, must have suffered a concussion. "Let's get him into the American

Hospital overnight for observation," the doctor said in halting English. "By morning, maybe we will know more."

But there was a glitch: The American Hospital had no available room in its small pediatric division. Now what? The doctor urged us to take him right away to the Emergency Room of the Hôpital Necker. We had never heard of the place, but the doctor assured us that Necker was the finest children's hospital in Paris. He called a taxi, and a few minutes later we were carrying baby Justin into the ER. By this time, Eda and I were both in a state, and Justin was in such pain that we could barely hold him in our arms. And we still had no clue as to what was causing it

The people at the admitting desk were bureaucratic and a bit chilly: Who were we? Who had sent us? What was wrong with the baby? How would we pay the bill? Finally we were ushered into a small examination room and a young doctor came in to see us. He was a short, wiry fellow, with thick black hair and a warm, understanding manner. As he loosened Justin's wrappings, he spoke to us in English, with an accent I couldn't place. "Doctor," I said, "if you don't mind me asking, where are you from?"

"I am from Russia," he said. "But don't worry, Mr. Shoot-koff," he said with a twinkle in his eye. "I am Jewish, just like you."

The doctor did a very thorough examination, gently poking and prodding Justin, and by this time the little guy was calming down a bit; the surroundings must have been terrifying, but I think he sensed he was in capable hands. "Well," the doctor said, "I do not agree with your doctor's diagnosis of a concussion. There is nothing wrong with his head."

Eda and I were not sure whether this was comforting news or not. "Let me do one or two things more . . ." In a moment, the doctor had his answer: The baby was bleeding internally. The cause: an intussusception.

Both the English word and its French counterpart, *invagination*, were unknown to us, but it sounded scary in either language. As the doctor explained, it was a rare condition where the lower intestine gets twisted and telescoped into the upper intestine. In the worst cases, this causes internal bleeding and excruciating pain. And, yes, this was a very bad case. "I am very sorry," he said. "We have to operate. Tonight."

Operate? Tonight?

You can imagine how we felt. We had just arrived in a new country, in a new culture, and with a howling baby we had landed in a hospital we didn't know, with a doctor we didn't know, and he was telling us that our baby needed emergency surgery for an ailment that we had never even heard of. And this was after another doctor had diagnosed a head injury! We were thoroughly shaken, to say the least.

"Doctor," I said. "Please give us a moment to collect our thoughts."

"Of course," he said. "Meantime, I will contact the head of surgery."

In search of a second opinion, Eda called her friend Susie Tompkins in San Francisco. Susie's brother, Tommy Russell, was himself a surgeon, and in a flash Eda and Tommy were on the phone discussing what we should do. Tommy knew the Hôpital Necker well, and it turned out he also knew the head surgeon, Dr. Yann Révillon. "Good man," Tommy assured us. "You're in good hands. If they say operate, you really have no other choice."

And so it was. The next few hours were some of the longest of our lives. Justin was admitted to the hospital and prepped for surgery. Then he went under the knife. Dr. Révillon opened Justin's stomach, put his intestines back into proper position, and took out his appendix, too—a normal practice with intussusception. Throughout the surgery, Eda and I were kept far away from the operating room and the doctors and nurses. The French attitude was, "This is our business, not yours. You need to stay as far away as possible so we can do our job."

Afterward, Dr. Révillon came out to tell us that everything had gone well. "We will need to keep him here, though, for another week," he said. "He will be fed through a tube until his stomach heals. After that, he will be good as new."

Then he said, "You know, we were lucky. If this had gone undiagnosed, even overnight, we might have lost him."

Around dawn they brought Justin up from the recovery room and put him in a tiny bed in the Intensive Care Unit. Eda and I were still not allowed anywhere near him; we could only watch him through a plate-glass window. And it was awful to see: Our little boy had an IV stuck into his head, and the nurses had pinned his arms to the bed, so he couldn't yank out the IV and do himself damage. Understandably, his mom was a wreck. Eda was used to holding him, feeding him, nursing him, keeping him warm. Now he was pinned to a cold hospital bed and there was nothing we could do to help or comfort him. All we could do was wait.

When Eda and I finally got home that morning, there was Zelda, worried sick. In certain realms, I know that dogs are far smarter and far more intuitive than we imagine they are; at least that was true in Zelda's case. When we arrived home without Justin, I felt absolutely sure that Zelda understood the state of anguish we were in. We couldn't hug Justin, but we sure hugged our little Zelda, and when we finally got to bed, she insisted on sleeping right at the foot.

Eda and I remained in anguish until the day we brought Justin home—and then it happened all over again. A day or two later, Justin started howling again. We rushed him back to Necker only to find out that he was suffering from a complication from the surgery; the doctors had to go back in and straighten his intestine again. This was every parent's nightmare: Your child is in distress, with nothing you can do to help. In response, Eda and I held each other close and prayed for the best, with Zelda again offering us all of her warmth and comfort. During this time, the bond we had with Zelda grew even tighter.

Justin came through like a champ. And this time when we got him home, we found something surprising: The little guy seemed changed; his natural development seemed to have accelerated. Maybe it was just our sense of relief, but Justin suddenly seemed older, more mature, more awake to his surroundings and to life itself. Eda and I certainly were. The ordeal had been a stunning lesson in the fragility of life: One moment your baby is happy and healthy, the next he's howling in pain and fighting to survive. And how ironic: In the shambles of India, we had rarely felt fear; in the luxury of Paris, it had come straight to our door.

Once again, though, Zelda was the perfect comic relief.

Our new apartment was on the ground floor, and the windows in the living room looked out to a lovely communal courtyard. There were two circles of grass in the middle and charming cobblestone walkways that led from the street to the four separate entrances of the apartment complex. The windows in our living room each had a mini-veranda, enclosed by an elegant iron railing and just the right size for a planter—and for Zelda. The veranda became her favorite perch. She would curl up at the base and take a nap in the sun, or stand up on her hind legs, with her paws poised on the top of the railing. From that position, standing on her hind legs—exactly as J.C. had captured her on the top of the pizza box—Zelda would greet all of our neighbors and any delivery man who came into our courtyard. Zelda now had a job: She was both a sentinel and an ambassador, greeting our neighbors and visitors with either a low, wary growl or, in most cases, murmurs of delight.

Our neighbors were not amused. *Ces Américains*, they sneered behind our backs. These Americans, bringing in a dog like that! They'll ruin the neighborhood! The great exceptions were the Pellissons: Jean-Claude, his wife, Monique, and their delightful daughters, Virginie and Delphine. We had an immediate bond with the Pellissons: They too had a dog, a gentlemanly rottweiler named Mec. In the morning and again in the evening, Jean-Claude or one of the girls would take Mec for a stroll, and this often entailed a joyous rendezvous with Zelda. Dogs, we were happy to discover, were as effective a social lubricant in France as they were in America.

Through Mec and Zelda, we quickly became friends with the Pellissons, but Zelda being Zelda, our new friendship came with an inexplicable quirk: Whenever she saw Virginie, Zelda would lose all control and immediately put down a puddle of pee. Outside in the courtyard or inside our apartment—it didn't matter where. For us, this was terribly embarrassing, but the Pellissons were amused and very understanding: They accepted Zelda for just what she was, an exotic, somewhat uncouth beast from the backstreets of India, bringing to our lives a healthy dose of spirit and sass.

The rest of our neighbors on the rue du Val de Grâce were not so forgiving. If a squirrel had the temerity to come browsing around our communal courtyard, Zelda would often take it upon herself to jump over the railing and chase it up the nearest tree. I'm sure that in Zelda's mind she was performing a public service, but the sniffiest of our neighbors would be outraged and make formal complaints to our concierge. How dare she upset the natural wildlife in our courtyard! Each time it happened, we would profusely apologize and swear up and down that it would never happen again. Not until the next time, anyway.

Taking Zelda for a walk in the neighborhood was equally amusing. On the corner of the rue du Val de Grâce was Madame Collin, who ran the neighborhood bakery and served as the unofficial mayor, fixer, and *Daily Bugle* of our quartier. She was a wonderful woman and a true institution. If you needed a plumber, Madame Collin had the man.

If you heard a delicious rumor about the couple next door, Madame Collin always had the inside scoop. I particularly admired the way she treated the kids in the neighborhood. It was part of their daily routine to stop in for a *croissant beurre*, a *pain au chocolat*, an apple turnover, or a bar of chocolate. But if a child was in any way misbehaving or impolite, Madame Collin at once became Miss Manners or Mother Superior: Not here, young man! Not in my store! Out! *Vamoose!*

Being an early riser, I often took Zelda for a brisk morning walk, and I often stopped in at Madame Collin's for a fresh baguette, hot from her husband's ovens, plus three or four of the warm croissants that Eda and I loved with our morning coffee. For fear of what she might do inside the bakery, I always left Zelda outside, her leash securely tied around the parking sign out front. But Madame Collin had a soft spot for our little girl, and with a wink she would often slip me a butter cookie or a madeleine as a treat for Zelda. I often wondered if Proust would approve.

Walking Zelda later in the day was far more complicated, especially if Eda or I had Justin riding on our back in his handy kid chair. The worst were the butcher shops. On the rue St. Jacques, one of the main shopping streets in our quartier, there were two butcher shops, one near Madame Collin, the other farther up the street. The second dealt in horse meat, but to Zelda that made no difference: Just as with the Pig Po back in Jor Bagh, she adamantly refused to pass in front of either one. And we were never sure where she would stop and refuse to budge. Sometimes it was a few steps from the butcher's door; other times it was fifty paces away. So we might have our arms loaded with grocery bags, with Justin on our back, and Zelda would abruptly stop or even turn tail and try to run away, dragging us behind her. To us, this was hysterically funny, but our neighbors were appalled. Fortunately, Eda was a very attractive woman and Justin was a handsome boy, with beautiful blond hair and an easy smile; otherwise we would have been instantly vilified as those awful Americans living on the rue du Val de Grâce.

Zelda did have one huge fan in our quartier: Raymond Aron. In France and in much of Europe, Raymond Aron was a revered figure. A distinguished philosopher, author, university professor, and a hero of the Resistance, Monsieur Aron was also our landlord, and every month I made it a point to go to his apartment on the Boulevard St. Michel and deliver the rent check in person. At that time, Monsieur Aron was writing a weekly column for *L'Express*, the French newsweekly, and he wrote at home, in his pajamas and robe. To deliver the rent, I would always call first, of course, but when I arrived at Monsieur Aron's door, he was often still in his robe and slippers. Then we would sit down and discuss French politics, or American foreign policy, or the consuming passion he shared with his grandson: the French national soccer team.

On one of my first visits to Monsieur Aron, I walked from our place around the corner to his and I brought Zelda along with me, assuming I would simply deliver the check and be on my way. But no. Monsieur Aron was in the mood to chat, and he invited Zelda and me into his parlor. Oh boy, this is going to be an adventure, I thought. I hope to heaven my little girl behaves herself. Well, she did better than that. Once we had settled in and Monsieur Aron was complaining about the power vacuum that he perceived at the time in Washington, D.C., Zelda crept slowly and quietly across the carpet and rested her head on the great man's slippers. I feared he might be annoyed, but he reached down and scratched her ears just the way she loved, and on the spot the two of them became fast friends. The rest of the neighborhood might turn up their noses and flee from her in droves, but Zelda had the eminent Raymond Aron and the Pellissons in her corner, and that was good enough for me.

In my unbridled love of dogs, I had another soul brother in Paris: Mort Rosenblum, the AP bureau chief in Paris. For more than a decade, Mort had been roaming the world for the AP, moving from hot spot to hot spot and building himself a big reputation, and on many of his travels he had in tow an exotic companion, O.B., his devoted German shepherd. In spirit and antics, O.B. had a touch of the Zelda: Her initials stood for "Odious Beast," and she frequently lived up to the name.

During our second autumn in Paris, Mort decided to throw a big Thanksgiving party at his apartment, and he invited us and a group of other Americans in Paris. It was a wonderful bash, and Mort laid out a sumptuous buffet: two turkeys, big bowls of stuffing, cranberry sauce, sweet potatoes, pecan and pumpkin pies—the works. Eda and I were there with Justin, who was now eighteen months old and quite the little gent. For this occasion, Mort very wisely kept O.B. locked in a back bedroom, but his girlfriend of the moment also had a German shepherd, Maxwell, and he was allowed to roam free. Maxwell was now going from guest to guest, nosing everyone and looking for handouts. Eda and I were sitting on a couch in the corner, eating from plates in our laps and helping Justin with his. Justin absolutely adored the roasted turkey and was busy gobbling down small bites with his fingers. Then, just as he was about to pop another bite in his mouth, Maxwell suddenly lunged in to grab it.

Wham!

Going for the turkey, Maxwell missed and sunk one of his long front teeth into Justin's upper lip, puncturing the skin and driving down deep. Justin leapt back, stunned, and suddenly blood began spouting from his lip like a geyser. He was almost too shocked to cry; Zelda had never given him a moment's fright. Eda and I swung into action, clamping my handkerchief onto Justin's lip to try to stop the bleeding. In an instant, though, my handkerchief was soaked with blood. Eda and I knew exactly what that meant: a trip back to the Emergency Room.

Mort was livid. Apparently he and his lady had argued about her dog even before the party started, and now the worst had come to pass. The two of them now resumed their battle, and Maxwell was banished to a back room. But an uneasy quiet now settled over the party. I asked Mort to please call us a taxi, but that was out of the question: He would drive us to the hospital himself and make sure that Justin was okay. Good man.

At that time Mort had a smart two-seater Fiat, with a tiny jump seat in the back. Mort got behind the wheel, Eda got into the front seat next to him, and I scrunched into the back with Justin in my arms and my hand still clamped on his lip, with several cloth napkins to absorb the blood. No one said a word. This was no one's idea of a happy Thanksgiving.

Even in the best of times, Mort was tightly coiled, ready to pounce; now he was ready to kill. He raced through the streets of Paris, weaving through traffic, barking at meandering drivers, determined to get us to the ER in record time. Given his embarrassment and worry, he felt that was the least he could do. Mort sped through one red light and was about to burn through another, but the car in front of us pulled up short and Mort had no choice but to slam on his brakes. Then we sat there in an uneasy silence, waiting for the light to finally turn green. At that moment, Justin let out a long, languorous sigh and said, "Ah, dog . . ."

Yes, "Ah, dog . . ."

At once all the tension in the car evaporated, and Eda, Mort, and I burst out laughing. There was a kind of weary wisdom in Justin's sigh, a philosophical acceptance that this was just one of those vicissitudes of life that seemed important now but soon would pass. It was as if he were saying to Eda and me, "Guys, relax. I've been through far worse, if you recall, and I came through just fine. Next to that, this is nothing at all!"

Yes, and Justin came through fine again: A few stitches in his lip and he was ready to go. In fact, if he had had his way, the little guy would have gone straight back to Mort's for more turkey and a few slices of pie.

From that night forward, that expression "Ah, dog," became for us far more than a cherished Paris memory; it became an outlook on life, an instant way for all of us to regain our humor and composure when everyone around us was flying into a tizzy. Now, whenever Zelda pulled one of her crazy stunts and the entire neighborhood was going up in arms, I would just sigh and say with a weary tone, "Ah, dog." And when Mort and I would be working in the AP bureau, covering some new terrorist attack or some grave political crisis, when the fate of civilization itself seemed to hang in the balance, we would look up from our keyboards and say with a sigh, "Ah, dog," and soon all would be right with the world.

CHAPTER EIGHT

Catcher in the Wry

France being France, food now took over our lives.

Every day became a gourmet immersion. For breakfast we would settle for nothing less than fresh croissants or baguettes from Madame Collin, preferably still warm from the oven. For lunch, we would never settle for a grilled cheese or a ham on rye; it had to be a proper, healthy three-course meal, with a fancy pâté to start, a main course running the gamut from a hearty *boeuf bourguignon* to a humble *steak frites*, and for dessert, at a bare minimum, we had to have a crème caramel, a *mousse au chocolat,* or a generous slice of Camembert, but only if it was *bien fait,* properly ripened, and preferably served with a slice of apple or a cluster of grapes—provided the grapes were plump, juicy, and straight from the vine.

Yes, overnight we became revolting snobs.

To the outside eye, this might sound like a delicious indulgence or, at worst, a minor affliction. But as Eda and I soon discovered, becoming a food snob is not a harmless by-product of living in France, not when you are trying your level best to raise happy, well-balanced children and dogs. Eda and I felt we were constantly facing a rampaging virus, out to infect our little ones and permanently skew their values and maim their lives. At times I saw myself as Holden Caulfield, running left and right, trying desperately to protect the innocent children from falling over the gourmet cliff.

With Justin, we saw the dangers early on. When he was a baby, Eda bought a wondrous little machine at a Paris kitchen shop: a small, plastic, tube-like contraption with a hand crank on the top. A food processor for babies. Eda would boil vegetables, make a little rice, maybe add in a few bits of chicken or hamburger, and then she would stuff them all down into the tube, crank the handle, and—*presto!*—homemade baby food fit for a king. Eda's intentions were admirable and this was a fine beginning.

On this foundation, young Justin developed a healthy appetite, and he was omnivorous in his taste. By the time he was four, Justin could go to La Coupole and down a dozen oysters, or he could go to a Burger King and wolf down a Whopper, consuming both with gusto and appreciation. Still, just by living and eating in Paris, Justin developed a palate that was not always easy to please. For instance, French moms often made for their kids *hachis parmentier*, a hearty peasant casserole made of hacked meat and mashed potatoes, and Justin loved it—provided it was not too heavy on the garlic. Likewise, he loved *mousse au chocolat*, but with a caveat or two. At one holiday dinner, our French hostess—a very accomplished cook—brought out a chocolate mousse she had made from her own special recipe, and while the rest of her guests at the table politely oohed and aahed over her creation, Justin, aged five, gagged and spit the stuff out. "Too much coffee!" he proclaimed. And he was right.

Now, you might expect some of the other guests at the table to be absolutely appalled at Justin's outburst, with a few murmuring under their breath, "The snotty little so-and-so! Who in the blazes does he think he is?" But no, this was France, and far from being appalled, the other guests at the table applauded our little gourmet-in-the-making. He was discerning. He was discriminating. His palate was *très raffiné*, very refined! Eda and I were at first baffled by their response, but we soon discovered that many of Justin's French playmates had been schooled to be even harsher in their food critiques. Eda was, by any standard, a first-rate cook, and her repertoire of fine dishes stretched from her native New Mexico to India and now to France. For lunch one winter day, she made an exquisite potato and leek soup and set it before Justin and one of his pals. "So, how do you like the soup, Jean-Pierre?"

"*Pas terrible*," was the withering reply. Not terrible. Passable.

This may sound like a small example of manners at the table, but it is illustrative of something much larger and more important in the French character: *l'esprit critique*. The critical spirit. Young or old, Parisian or peasant, no self-respecting French man or woman will ever go along with the crowd; that would be the sign of an uncritical mind and of an intolerable mediocrity in both judgment and taste.

"How do you like the Picasso, Justin?"

"Wow, cool!"

"And how do you like the Picasso, Jean-Pierre?"

"*Pas terrible*."

In France, whether it is about food or wine, painting or movies, politics or world affairs, there are few exceptions: *L'esprit critique* rules the day. And in France it all starts at the family table. French parents, we soon discovered, actually encourage their children to become revolting food snobs;

that instantly sets them above the riffraff, meaning above everyone else. Justin's *mousse au chocolat* episode did give us cause for concern, but later on we received some reassuring news. At that time, we had a wonderful American au pair helping us, Ellen Speroni, and one day Ellen's brother Teddy arrived from the States, bringing with him something that Justin had never seen before: a bag of Oreo cookies. Justin opened the bag, took out a cookie, and then instinctively twisted open the cookie and licked out the filling. Wow! Somehow the kid knew exactly how to eat an Oreo cookie; we figured it must be wired into his all-American genes. From that point on, Eda and I knew that while Justin would be discerning in his taste, he would never fully succumb to the deadly food-snob virus.

Ethan was a whole other story.

Two and a half years after Justin was born in India, Ethan, our second son, was born in the American Hospital of Paris. He arrived with much less strain on his mother, but he made up for that soon thereafter. Unlike Justin, Ethan did not cotton to the homogenized mush that came out of Eda's tubular food processor; he wanted to know exactly what he was putting into his mouth and stomach. And he didn't want anything passing his lips that tasted mundane. Even as a tiny baby, Ethan didn't want mashed potatoes or boiled carrots; he wanted mangoes and lychees and honeydew melon. By the age of two, he had developed an unbridled passion for escargot—provided there was plenty of garlic and lots of baguette to mop up the juices. We would take the little guy out to bistros for escargot and even the French would watch him in wonder. As he got older, Ethan's tastes became even more surprising. Give him a choice between a bowl of ice cream and a bowl of grapefruit, and he would choose the grapefruit every single time. Likewise, Ethan could go for weeks without touching meat, but if he was feeling a little listless and in need of a boost, he would down an entire rib eye steak and demand another. He loved foie gras too—at the age of four. Now you can see the dangers of raising kids in France.

Still, like Justin, Ethan never became a revolting food snob. He had a discerning palate, and he simply knew what he liked and what he didn't. And if he did not like whatever was the *plat du jour* at school or at home, he simply refused to eat it—and no amount of parental cajoling or bribery could make him change his mind. At the tender age of eighteen months, in fact, Ethan formally laid down the law. One night Eda steamed some fresh green peas and placed a few of them on Ethan's plate. Peas? No way. Ethan wouldn't touch them. Refusing to take his no for an answer, Eda stuffed a few peas into a spoonful of mashed potatoes and then she waved the spoon in the air, mimicking the movement of a jet airplane coming in for a landing. "Here it comes, open wide," she said in her most enticing voice. But as soon as that spoon came near his lips, Ethan swatted it away and issued his decree: "I decide what I eat!" Yes, that was Ethan, then as now. Peas be damned, I decide what I eat!

And that brings us directly to Zelda.

When we first arrived in Paris, Eda continued Sheela's tradition of cooking huge pots of food for Zelda, using various meats, vegetables, rice, or spaghetti and providing Zelda with enough home-cooked food to last for a week or more. But after Ethan was born, Eda had her hands full with two young boys, plus she was learning legal French, studying for the French bar exam, and getting ready for the day she would go back to work as a lawyer. With so much to handle, doing special shopping and cooking for Zelda was a substantial drain on her time and energy. Still, Eda was happy to do it—until one day a family friend suggested she was more than a bit out of her mind. "Eda," she said, "if you keep cooking for that dog, you'll be stuck cooking for her for the rest of her life—and for far too much of yours!"

Thus began a rude chapter in the life of Zelda: the Battle of Paris. Eda's mind was now made up: She had cooked her last meal for Zelda; we had to wean our little princess to regular dog food. So we went out and bought a twenty-five-pound bag of kibble, what we were assured was the very best brand that France had to offer. Zelda wouldn't go near it. The kibble would stay in her bowl, untouched, for days on end. Okay, we said, let's do this more gradually: We'll mix the kibble with a generous helping of Eda's home-cooked stew, until Zelda grows accustomed to it, and then in a week or two we can wean her down to just the kibble. That ought to work, right?

Ha! Zelda would have none of it. To her, the resultant mix was still kibble, just barely disguised. So we shifted strategy once again, this time splurging on what was billed as the filet mignon of French dog food. This was a canned food that featured top-quality vegetables and the finest of meats, no gristle. It was, we were assured, food fit for even the fussiest of French poodles. We opened the can and to our noses the food seemed moist and delectable enough, but when we filled Zelda's bowl and set it before her, our little princess practically laughed in our faces. It was just like Ethan with those peas: Me, eat that? Are you out of your bleeping minds?

Eda was furious. Zelda, after all, had started out life as a filthy street dog in India, scrounging through gutters and eating garbage of the foulest sort. And now in Paris she wouldn't eat kibble? Or the best canned food from the kitchens of gourmet France? Come on now, enough is enough! Stop being such a spoiled little princess! Still, always trying to be sensitive and understanding toward our little girl, Eda and I wondered whether there might be some calm, rational explanation for Zelda's refusal to eat processed dog food. Might there be some hidden link to her violent reaction to any and all butcher shops? Was there something, perhaps, in the smell of the meat that made her nauseous?

But then we noticed something else: Zelda had taken a shine to Camembert cheese. She absolutely adored it. But if the Camembert was not *bien fait*, properly ripened, we found that Zelda would either eat it begrudgingly or not touch it at all. Likewise, at breakfast she begged for a taste of the warm croissants that I brought home from Madame Collin. Fine. That was only natural; the croissants were sinfully good. But then an American-style supermarket opened right down the street, and there we found something entirely new to France: a six-pack of croissants, made industrially, wrapped in plastic, and baked Lord only knew when. Yes, Son of Wonder Bread had come to France. A sad day, to say the least. Still, the price was irresistible, so we bought a six-pack, took it home, and then we heated up all six, including a whole croissant for Zelda, the lucky dog. But when we presented it to her, warm from the oven, Zelda arrogantly turned up her nose and refused to touch it. Then and there Eda and I had to admit the awful truth:

Zelda had become a revolting food snob.

Yes, it was true. Justin and Ethan had suffered only mild strains of the virus, but our poor Zellie had come down with a full-blown case. Eda and I were consumed with guilt. Was France to blame? Or were we to blame, always cooking special meals for her and indulging our spoiled little princess? Either way, Eda and I now faced a painful dilemma: What do we do now? How do we unspoil a very spoiled girl? Do we bury our heads and ignore the issue? Do we give in, put away the kibble and canned food, and resume cooking for Zelda her homemade stews? Here Eda was absolutely adamant: No way. Give in now and her friend would be right: She'd be cooking for Zelda for the rest of her life. Eda's mind was made up: We had to be ruthless. No more half measures, no more pussyfooting around. Our little angel was infected, and Eda saw only one possible cure: Break her. And like it or not, we had to do it the hard way:

Cold kibble.

Now the Battle of Paris began in earnest. Each morning Eda would put out a fresh bowl of kibble and in a firm but motherly way tell Zelda: "Eat! This is all you get from here on out!" No more home-cooked meals, no more Camembert, no more croissants. Period. Finished. End of story. And no room for appeal. This was a side of Eda that I had never seen before. Gone was the soft, forgiving, animal-loving heart. This was the Stern, Parental, No-Nonsense Eda. This was the Tough-Love Eda. This was the Don't-You-Dare-Mess-With-Me-Sister Eda. I was very impressed.

Zelda, undaunted, went on a hunger strike.

Each morning Eda would put out a fresh bowl of kibble, and each morning Zelda very proudly refused to go near it. This went on for days and weeks; Zelda was subsisting on water and blades of grass or discarded crêpes she found on our walks in the Luxembourg Gardens. "If I can survive in the streets of India," she seemed to say, "by golly I can survive quite well, thank you, on the rue du Val de Grâce!" At times, Zelda would even shoot me a sly little grin: "Break me? Ha, I'll show her!"

I can't tell you how much fun this was for me, watching this battle of wills, watching these two smart, stubborn women go to the mat. The Comédie Française and the Paris Opera had nothing to match it. And I had to admire both of them. Eda was being the stern, responsible parent, setting clear boundaries and enforcing them, and Zelda was showing us her true character and mettle. "My begging days are over!" she almost cried. "This is Paris! I'm a princess now! And I will *not* be deprived!"

While I was amused, Justin and Ethan were both getting extremely anxious: "Mommy, Zeldie's still not eating. Shouldn't we give her some different food? She must be very, very hungry after all this time."

But Eda, bless her, would not budge. She would show this beast who was the boss! This battle of wills went on for weeks—more than some shows last on Broadway—and Zelda kept getting thinner and thinner. Finally, responding to an insistent wail from her animal-loving heart, Eda gave in, but only an inch. She went to the store and came back with five different kinds of canned dog food, looking for some brand that Zelda would accept—and looking, too, for a graceful way to beat a retreat.

Eda found the answer in Canigou, a canned dog food that actually looked a bit like *boeuf bourguignon*. I say "looked," not smelled. To my nose, it smelled downright disgusting, but Zelda gave in and decided to eat it, albeit reluctantly. Success! Eda was now able to claim a victory of sorts: She would no longer be spending hours and hours each week cooking special meals for her very spoiled child. And Zelda was able to claim a victory, too: She had made it perfectly clear, to one and all, that kibble in any form was now totally beneath her new station in life. So the two of them finally kissed and made up, and we were able to call it a draw. In Zelda's head, though, I could see this was only a tactical retreat. This was gourmet France; she would keep her powder dry and live to gorge another day. And that day came much sooner than I expected . . .

At his local school around the corner, Justin had made a friend, Nicolas Zylberstein, and we had become friends with Nicolas's parents, Marie-Christine and Jean-Claude.

The Zylbersteins had a lovely weekend home in the country in a tiny village called Le Mesnil-Théribus, about an hour's drive north of Paris, and one weekend they invited us to come out and join them. We did, with Zelda happily in tow. Both families had a wonderful time. Justin played soccer and board games with Nicolas, and Ethan had fun riding bikes and playing on the swings with Julien, Nicolas's younger brother. So it was a good fit all around, and soon Eda and Marie-Christine turned those relaxing weekends in the country into a regular feature of our Paris life—until Zelda threatened to ruin it all.

The country house had been in Marie-Christine's family for years, and in the field out back they kept a small herd of sheep. The animals were sweet, docile, and easy to maintain, and by the end of winter they would always be loaded with beautiful white, fluffy wool. In our eyes, they were a perfect addition to a home in the country. Late one afternoon, though, when no one was looking, Zelda sneaked out into the field and went berserk. Just as she used to run around me in the park back in Jor Bagh, she now ran around and around the sheep, nipping them in the bottom and herding them into a tight little ball. If a sheep dared to go astray, Zelda would nip at its ankles and drive it back into line. In a minute or two, the sheep were thoroughly terrorized and Zelda had wads of wool streaming from her jaws.

This was a stunning turn of events. Some primal instinct, coming from God knows where—Zelda had never seen a sheep before—had seized our little girl and turned her into an unchained menace, a big, unruly sheep dog hell-bent to herd!

Marie-Christine was not pleased, to say the least. When she and Eda heard the commotion, they ran out into the field and managed to chase Zelda away. As soon as she came back to her senses, Zelda tucked her tail between her legs and slinked away. But the damage was done: One of the lambs was badly mangled. And there was no saving her. Marie-Christine came back with a shotgun and put her out of her misery.

Zelda's stunt could have meant the end of a beautiful friendship. But Marie-Christine and Jean-Claude were remarkably understanding, Zelda was adorably contrite, sulking around in shame, and soon all was forgiven. With that, our idyllic weekends in the country continued, but not without a surprising twist. Alongside her Camembert and croissants, Zelda now added another gourmet craving: borscht.

Yes, borscht. Marie-Christine's mother came from a Jewish family in Poland, and she had brought with her to France an old family recipe for borscht. And Marie-Christine's version of it was marvelous. She used fresh beets, onions, and chives from her own garden, crème fraîche from one of the farmers in the neighborhood, and bits of lamb from a freshly slaughtered sheep. (Yes, that sheep; Marie-Christine kept the meat in her freezer.) One night Marie-Christine was ladling out her borscht to the rest of us, and our little Zelda came to the table begging for a taste.

Right away, Eda snapped to attention. And I knew why. The last thing in the world she wanted was for Zelda to have a taste of that enticing borscht. By now, our Zelda had finally come to accept her Canigou, and Eda was adamant: There were to be no more special meals for our revolting food snob, and she would brook no weakening or slippage in this regard. That was a fine policy. But what could Eda do now, sitting at the Zylberstein's family table? We were guests in their home, our kids were the best of pals, and if Eda put her foot down and insulted our hostess, all of our weekends in the country and all of our friendship and good cheer might now come to a screeching halt.

Zelda, though, was not to be denied. Using all her charm and guile, she edged in close to Marie-Christine, the aroma of that borscht dancing in her nostrils. Usually Marie-Christine would simply shush her away from the table, but not tonight. Looking into Zelda's eyes, seeing her crave just a little taste, Marie-Christine took out one of her finest china bowls, then dipped her ladle into the tureen and gave it a swirl.

Poor Eda. She sat there frozen in her chair, torn in two. One part of her wanted to scream out, "No borscht! It carries the virus!" while the other part of her shrunk from doing anything that might offend our hosts. All she could do was watch in horror as Marie-Christine filled that lovely china bowl with her borscht and then set it down on the kitchen floor in front of our little Zelda. She even reached down and gave our girl a gentle pat on the head, as if to say, "Enjoy, *ma petite*. And welcome to the family."

On every other occasion, Zelda would just dive right in and scarf down that soup. But not now. Somehow she appreciated the importance of the moment, and she approached that bowl with great delicacy and care. From a respectful distance, she circled and sniffed the borscht, the way a French wine connoisseur might appraise a Burgundy from a very fine chateau. At last, she licked a corner of the bowl, and then, casting an approving eye back to Marie-Christine, she began to dig in.

Well now!

"Forget Camembert," Zelda seemed to say, smacking her lips as she ate, "and don't bother me with croissants; this borscht is simply divine!" In evident rapture, Zelda very slowly and appreciatively downed the rest of the bowl, savoring each and every lick, and then she came back and very politely begged for more. Marie-Christine was thrilled to oblige, delighted that our little girl was showing such breeding, such refinement and class. With even more joy than before, Zelda downed her second bowl of borscht, and we all could see Marie-Christine glow with satisfaction and pride.

At a single stroke, of course, the Battle of Paris was now brought to its close. From this point forward, Zelda would silently endure her Canigou, but only because glorious, borscht-filled weekends now frolicked on the horizon as far as her devilish little eye could see. Yes, Zelda the Gourmet Princess was back triumphant—and there was not a single word that Eda could say about it.

Victory, my friends, rarely tasted quite so sweet.

CHAPTER NINE

Intruder in the Dust

One spring morning I was in the Paris bureau of the Associated Press, looking for stories to write, when a courier arrived with our weekly celebrity tip sheet, put out by the Paris office of a Hollywood PR firm. I looked it over and one name immediately jumped up to my eyes: Hemingway.

Mariel Hemingway, a granddaughter of Ernest, was making her acting debut in a new film by Woody Allen, *Manhattan,* and she was going to stop in Paris on her way down to the Cannes Film Festival, where the film was to have its world premiere. "Hmmm," I said to myself, "a new generation of Hemingways coming to Paris; surely there's some sort of story in that . . ." Mariel, the tip sheet said, was arriving that night. Right away I called the PR firm and set up an interview for the very next morning.

At ten o'clock the following morning, I arrived at the Plaza Athenée, one of the finest hotels in Paris, located on the Avenue Montaigne, near the Champs-Elysées. I brought along with me Michel Lipschitz, one of the AP's best news and celebrity photographers. Between the two of us, I figured we could come up with a decent story or at least a good photo spread with some interesting captions regarding Mariel's arrival in Paris.

At the front desk, we asked for Miss Hemingway, and soon Michel and I were knocking on the big double door of a luxury suite. The door opened and there stood Ernest Hemingway, back from the grave. Our jaws dropped. It was Mariel's father, Jack, and he was the spitting image of his father: tall, handsome, muscular, with huge forearms, a white moustache, and an easy, radiant Big Country grin. Seeing our faces, Jack laughed and said, "Yeah, I get that all the time. The curse of the son . . ."

Mariel looked like anything but a budding Hollywood star. She was dressed in a T-shirt and faded jeans, and she looked like she was ready for her high school math class back home in Ketchum, Idaho, not for her world debut on the red carpets of Cannes. On top of that, she was all of seventeen and she had little to say. How was it, I asked, working with Woody Allen? "It was sooo cool! He made me feel really comfortable." Stop the presses!

What intrigued me much more was Jack. While I chatted with Mariel and Michel clicked madly away, Jack hovered close by, wanting on the one hand to protect his daughter and, on the other, to give her plenty of room to relax and shine. He was a dad, just like me and most every other dad I knew. A few minutes into the interview, I exchanged glances with Michel and he read my mind. "Miss Hemingway," I said, "I have an idea, if you don't mind. What if you went over to the Tuileries Gardens with Michel and then over to Notre Dame? He can get great stuff with you there."

"Cool!" she said, and I could see Dad quietly nod his approval.

While Mariel went off to change her clothes and Michel packed up his gear, I said to Jack, "You know, I'm a huge fan of your father's work."

"Really?"

"Yes, I did my senior thesis on him, comparing his work to Albert Camus's. I've read almost every word your father wrote."

"Huh," Jack said, and I could see the wheels turning in his head. "Listen," he said, "I had a quadruple bypass a few months ago, and my doc has ordered me to walk two hours a day. This afternoon I'm going to go out and see some of my old haunts in Paris. Wanna come along?"

How in the world could I ever say no?

I went back to the AP bureau and dashed off a few hundred words on Mariel's arrival in Paris. As I wrapped it up, Michel came rushing into the newsroom. "Paul, you won't believe it," he said. "This girl, she looks so plain in person, *n'est-ce pas*? But guess what? She has something very special, and the camera, it picks it up right away. The camera absolutely adores her. Woody Allen, he has a fantastic eye."

Michel and I grabbed a sandwich and then I headed right back to the Plaza Athenée. Jack was waiting. From his hotel, we walked down the Avenue Montaigne, crossed the river to the Left Bank, and then we walked along the other side of the Seine. Jack was soon in a wistful mood. When we came to the American Church, facing the river, he said, "This is where I got married, right after the war. Julia Child was our matron of honor."

What?

Yes, as Jack now explained, during the war he had worked for the OSS, the Office of Strategic Services, the precursor to the CIA. Having grown up in France, he spoke impeccable French, and during the war he passed himself off as French and worked undercover, helping to organize the French Resistance. Julia Child also worked for the OSS, and during that period the two became close friends. The common wisdom today is that Julia worked only in the administrative offices of the OSS, but Jack intimated that her role involved more serious derring-do. Either way, this was all news to me, and as we walked I took copious mental notes.

From the river, we cut in along the Boulevard St. Germain, and soon we were heading up the Boulevard Raspail and past the foot of the rue de Fleurus. Gertrude Stein had lived at 27 rue de Fleurus, and when Jack was tiny, his dad and mom, Ernest's first wife, Hadley, often deposited "Mister Bumby," as they affectionately called him, with Miss Stein and Alice B. Toklas, using them as babysitters when Ernest and Hadley wanted a night on the town. Jack told me about that as we walked, and he also told me many very personal stories, both about his father and about how difficult it had been living in his father's monstrous shadow. Jack and his wife, Puck, had three beautiful, accomplished daughters—Mariel, her actress sister Margaux, and Muffet, the oldest—but that only complicated his burden: "You know," Jack confided to me, "I've always been somebody's son or somebody's father. I've never been me."

Our final destination was one of his father's favorite cafes, the Closeries des Lilas, located at the southern tip of the Luxembourg Gardens, just a few blocks from our front door. The Closeries had a small bronze plaque in the bar, in honor of Ernest. On this splendid spring afternoon, warm and breezy, Jack and I sat out on the terrace of the Closeries, drinking pastis, reminiscing, and watching the light of the day soften and slowly disappear. I was in literary heaven: This was *A Moveable Feast* sprung to life, with "Bumby," the oldest of Ernest's three sons, sitting beside me and telling me stories about his dad and mom, about Pablo Picasso, Scott and Zelda Fitzgerald, and many of the other writers and painters he had known growing up in the Paris of the Roaring Twenties.

Like his father, Jack was an avid fly fisherman, and out on the terrace he told me that on a recent trip to Paris he had gone to a fishing store that he had heard about in the Place Wagram, not far from the Arc de Triomphe. The store featured racks and racks of fabulous hand-tied flies, all of them expertly crafted and many in designs and colors that Jack had never seen before. Jack was so excited that he bought scores and scores of flies—at a cost far beyond the amount of French francs he had in his wallet. At the cash register, Jack was a little sheepish. "Pardon me," he asked the owner, "but by any chance do you take credit cards?"

"*Mais oui*," the owner said.

Jack handed him his Visa card, and the owner was intrigued by the name on the card. "Hemingway," he said. "Any relation to Ernest?"

"Why, yes. I'm his firstborn son."

With that, the owner reached out his hand. "Sasha Tolstoy," he said. "Grandson of Leo. Pleased to meet you!"

Jack and I sat and talked until well after 11 p.m., and as soon as we said good-bye, I dashed home and typed all of my mental notes out onto paper. The next day I wrote a long story for the AP describing our time together and turning it into an intimate profile of Jack. The story ran in newspapers all over the world, and through this encounter Jack and I became good friends. When he came back to Paris the following summer, Eda invited him to join us for dinner at the house, nothing fancy, just a simple spaghetti meal and some time with us and our boys. At the appointed hour, Jack arrived at our door with two bottles of his favorite Burgundy, Chambolle-Musigny, and guess who came rushing to greet him.

"And who might this be?" Jack asked.

"This," I said, "is Zelda."

"Well," he said, with a huge Hemingway grin, "Zelda was a bitch!"

As you can see, the wild little beast we rescued from the streets of India was now leading quite the life in Paris: Her days were filled with Camembert, croissants, and literary hobnobbing, and her weekends in the country were filled with fresh goat cheese, homemade borscht, and the naughty temptation of terrorizing sheep. I think it is a safe bet that no street dog from the Indian subcontinent ever had it quite so good.

But Zelda's *vie en rose* still held a nasty barb: Many of our closest neighbors on the rue du Val de Grâce detested the very sight of her. Out on the street it wasn't so bad; the real problem was with the people who lived right in our own complex. And they had their reasons. Once or twice a week, Zelda would still vault out of our front window and chase a squirrel up a tree, and whenever she saw Virginie Pellisson and their dog, Mec, Zelda would still, almost on cue, release a large puddle of pee, often on the lovely cobblestones in front of our building. In the eyes of our neighbors, such antics were reprehensible, and they viewed Zelda as a blight on the entire complex and on their own personal quality of life. Eda and I felt it was futile to argue. And then Zelda did something even worse. Much worse.

The concierge of our complex lived with her husband in a cottage beside our front gate, and the couple had two young, high-spirited boys, Patrick and Joël. Zelda was usually polite and gentle with both of them, but Joël had a very annoying habit: He liked to yank on Zelda's tail, and sometimes he would even jump on her back and try to ride her like a pony. Most of the time, Zelda tolerated such intrusions with good humor, but if it got to be too much, she would warn Joël off with a gentle growl. One day, though, Joël was too revved up to listen, and after one tail yank too many, Zelda clamped her teeth down on Joël's forearm. It was not really a bite, and no skin was broken; Zelda was only trying to teach the boy a valuable lesson. Still, the howling that ensued could be heard, I'm sure, at the very top of the Eiffel Tower.

Eda and I were both mortified. As parents ourselves, we certainly understood the anger and concern of our concierge and her husband. We apologized profusely, showed them Zelda's rabies certificate, and we swore up and down that it would never, ever happen again. By nightfall, though, this was a full-blown scandal and the talk of the courtyard. *Ces Américains!* Those Americans! And that dog! That eyesore! That foul, uncouth little beast! *Insupportable!* Eda and I half-expected to see a petition start making the rounds, demanding our immediate ouster from the premises. Indeed, over the ensuing weeks, our neighbors, apart from the Pellissons, would not even speak to us, and when Zelda wandered by, they would lift their noses and treat her like a complete pariah.

But Zelda would soon have her day.

One night around 1:30 a.m., Zelda came into our bedroom and nudged my hand with her nose. She also made a strange mewling sound, to show me that she was very upset. I was sound asleep when she nudged me; I told her to shush and leave us alone. A minute later, though, Zelda was back, and just to appease her I got up, checked the windows, the front door, and the back door that led to our small interior courtyard. Nothing was awry. "Satisfied now?" I said, and climbed back into bed.

A minute later, though, Zelda was back in our bedroom. Eda was now very annoyed. "Zelda, go back to bed!" she said. "Now!"

Zelda slinked off, but a minute and a half later she came right back. This time she jumped up onto my side of the bed, draped her front legs across my chest, and then relentlessly jabbed her nose into my belly.

"Okay, okay," I said. "I'll have another look . . ."

This time I put on a robe, checked the kids, checked the kitchen, and checked the door to the courtyard out back. Still no sign of anything amiss. Then I opened our front door, checked the entryway, and checked the stairs that led up five flights to the top of our building: still nothing. Everything seemed to be in order. As one last precaution, I opened the door to the stairs that led down to the cellar. Above ground, our building had a lovely, sophisticated feel, but when you went down into the cellar, it looked and felt like a medieval dungeon: It was dark, drafty, and filled with dust. Each apartment in the building had its own individual storage unit down there, and the lighting in the cellar was especially poor, so we always had to take a flashlight with us when we went down to retrieve an empty suitcase or a can of paint.

I made my way to the bottom of the cellar stairs and then peered up and down the narrow rows of storage units. On the left and on the right, everything seemed to be buttoned up tight. But as I headed back up, from a far corner of the cellar I heard a strange noise, a cold metallic *snap*! And then again: *snap*! There was no mistaking the sound: Someone was snapping the padlocks and breaking into the storage units. I quietly crept back upstairs, went inside, double-locked the door, and called the cops.

In just a few minutes, two squad cars pulled up at our gate and four French cops came rushing into the courtyard. I met them at the entrance to our building, explained the situation, and then led them to the top of the stairs leading down to the cellar. In mere moments the cops apprehended the burglar, without a struggle, and a second team quickly nabbed his girlfriend; she was waiting for him in a car parked just down the street. Then we got the big surprise: This was no hum-drum burglar; this was a *wine* burglar. And a very knowledgeable wine burglar at that. He was snapping padlocks, grabbing empty suitcases, and then filling them with only the finest chateau wines, many of them heirloom Burgundies and Bordeaux that had been in our neighbors' families for years and some for generations. I had to laugh: a wine burglar! Where else but France?

By morning, the whole courtyard was abuzz, and Madame Collin, the *Daily Bugle* of Val de Grâce, was trumpeting the news: Indian Dog Captures Wine Burglar! Hear all about it! *Vive Zelda! Vive La France!*

By noontime, Zelda was the toast of the neighborhood. The mailman, the butcher, the flower lady—everyone was talking about Zelda and applauding her keen nose, her perspicacity, her tenaciousness, even her fine manners and exceptional breeding. By evening, even our sniffiest neighbors were singing her praises; they had been to police headquarters and had seen for themselves the burglar's haul: scores of Burgundies and Bordeaux, a booty worth thousands of dollars on the black market and even more in sentimental value. The loss to our Parisian neighbors would have been incalculable, but our little Zelda had saved the day—and their family treasures.

To show their undying appreciation, to properly salute this humble heroine in their midst, our neighbors now set before our Zelda a raft of glittering riches: huge roast beef bones direct from the butcher, exquisite leather collars and leashes from the finest pet shops in Paris, and doggie toys and treats more fit for display at the Louvre than for canine consumption.

Most important, a full redemption was now at hand. All of Zelda's earlier antics and transgressions were now magically erased, and yesterday's pariah from the streets of India was now formally proclaimed, by one and by all, the Queen of Paris. All our little Zelda lacked now was the scepter, the jeweled tiara, and the idyllic summer palace beside the Mediterranean Sea.

This Side of Paradise

Zelda never turned into a French poodle.

Even after she was crowned the "Queen of Paris," even after our neighbors swathed her in gifts and gratitude for saving their precious wine collections, Zelda never became snotty or put on airs. On our walks through the Luxembourg Gardens, or when we stopped for a coffee or a glass of wine at a Paris cafe, Zelda could put her best paw forward and pass herself off as the very picture of European refinement and breeding, but deep down, in some irrepressible part of her being, she remained the high-spirited, impulsive Indian street girl, charming, capricious, and totally untamed, just as she had been born to be.

The instances were now few and far between, but on a warm spring day Zelda might still vault out the window and chase a squirrel or two up the nearest tree, or on weekends out in Mesnil, when no one was looking, she just might sneak out into the pasture and find a few hapless sheep to round up and herd into a ball. There was nothing malicious about her outbursts, and no further damage was ever done; this was just Zelda being Zelda, showing us that as cozy and comfortable as her life had become in Paris, every once in a while she had to cut loose and assert her independence, she had to thumb her nose at the proper manners and constrictions of bourgeois France and remember what it was like to be totally free.

Zelda's spirit was contagious.

We saw that early on with Ethan. One summer in Paris, when he was only three, we had a heat wave and Ethan found a satisfying way to cool himself down: He would lift Zelda's water bowl up over his head and then use it to give himself a shower. He splashed water all over himself and all over the floor—and enjoyed every second of it. At first Eda was amused and pleased by his display of ingenuity, but she soon tired of drying him off and mopping the floor. "Ethan," she said sternly, "no more!"

Soon, though, Ethan would be off playing, he'd get hot and sticky all over again, and then he would return to Zelda's water bowl for another refreshing shower. After three or four rounds of this, Eda became totally exasperated: "Ethan, that's enough! Look at the mess you made! If you do that again, I'm going to slap your hand!"

Well, such ultimatums did not sit very well with Mr. I Decide What I Eat. An hour or so later, Ethan was once again hot and sticky and couldn't resist putting his mother to the test. He took Zelda's water bowl and gave himself another long, luxurious shower. Hearing the commotion, Eda stormed out of the kitchen: "Ethan Chutkow, what did I tell you?" With that, Ethan simply held out his hand, ready for his slap—it was a small price to pay for such an enjoyable crime. Eda did administer the punishment, but it was hard to do it and keep a straight face.

Zelda's untamed spirit affected all of us, including me. One morning I was in the AP bureau, reading the papers, when an urgent story came over the wire from Oslo, Norway: Mother Teresa had been awarded the Nobel Peace Prize. I immediately sat down and wrote an intimate profile of Mother, based in part on the time I had spent with her in Calcutta. But I wanted to do more. So I lobbied my AP colleagues and they readily agreed: I would go to Oslo to cover the actual awarding of the Peace Prize and the festivities that customarily surround it.

In some ways, being a foreign correspondent is like being a fireman: As soon as an earthquake or a plane crash occurs somewhere, you're on your way to the airport, laptop and tools in hand, prepared for the worst. This time was different. As soon as I boarded the Air France flight to Oslo, I had a feeling of elation: This was a story that would be positive and uplifting—for once. From the moment I had arrived in France, much of my time and energy had been spent covering acts of terror, malevolence, and hatred. In the name of this cause or that, terror groups were carrying out kidnappings, hijackings, bomb attacks, and assassinations, some right on the streets of Paris. This was not the best of times in the City of Light. I needed a break, I needed jolt of fresh, positive energy, and Oslo promised to provide just that.

I arrived in Oslo the night before the Nobel ceremony, and with our local AP man I had a lovely walk through the city. Then, in a charming cafe, we sat down to "lutefisk," a traditional Norwegian feast usually featuring dried cod or another white fish. My hopes were high, but the cod had a taste someplace between rat poison and turpentine, and the side dishes were worse: mushy green peas with chunks of greasy bacon, mashed rutabaga, mashed potatoes drowning in heavy brown gravy, and a lumpy, doughy concoction that Madame Collin would never dream of calling "bread." Of course, I had to be polite and rave about the lutefisk, an act of diplomacy made possible only by consuming industrial quantities of Akvavit, the Scandinavian equivalent of anti-freeze. Yes, I too could be a revolting food snob.

What the Norwegians may have lacked in culinary finesse, they more than made up for in dignity and class: The following day's Nobel Peace Prize ceremony was magnificent in every detail. The Norwegian royal family, the Norwegian Parliament (five members of which choose the Peace Prize recipient each year), and past Nobel laureates from around the world all gathered in a glittering hall to pay homage to Mother Teresa and her noble work among the poorest of the poor. When she stepped to the podium to receive the prize and give her acceptance speech, I could see that in dress and spirit, Mother remained exactly as she had been in Calcutta: totally humble in her presence, yet fiery in her intelligence and steel-like in her values. In her speech, Mother spoke about the privilege of serving the poor, and of course about the ever-present, all-knowing God who she said guided her every step. In jaded, materialist old Europe it was an unusual message to hear, and that tiny woman held the entire Nobel community in the palm of her hand.

Afterward, as she was meeting informally with a few members of the press, I discreetly approached Mother Teresa, wondering whether she might remember me; it had been over three years since I had spent time with her in Calcutta. Stupid me for doubting. As soon as I came up, she let out that playful chuckle of hers and wagged her finger at me: "You see, Paul, I told you we would see each other again!" Amazing woman. We had a brief private chat, then she said, "Will you be joining us tonight?"

"Yes, Mother. I wouldn't miss it for the world."

That night a huge crowd of people gathered in the wind and the bitter cold to walk with Mother Teresa through the streets of Oslo. They came from across Norway and other parts of Europe, and many came from India, too, all to honor Mother and voice their support for peace and better understanding among the different peoples of the world. Mother walked at the front of the crowd, clad in her usual leather sandals and her blue and white habit, with only wool socks and a heavy woolen shawl to protect her from the cold. At first, the crowd walked along in reverential silence, and then, spontaneously, people began to sing. In a meld of languages and lovely voices, they sang Christmas carols and spiritual hymns, and many held candles as they walked, their hands protecting the flame, tears streaming down their faces. What a spirit this woman had; what boundless faith and devotion she was able to inspire.

When I got back to Paris, I became extremely blue. Even though I was surrounded by the wonderful warmth of Eda, Justin, Ethan, and Zelda, and even though I was living my dream of being a writer in Paris, I was still feeling constrained and unfulfilled. Watching and writing about Mother Teresa forced me to confront the big question: What the heck was I doing with my life? Yes, through the power and global reach of the Associated Press, I was able to *inform* millions of people, a vital public service to be sure, but how many people had I ever *inspired*? Very few, if any. I still loved the adrenaline rush of covering international news, but after Oslo I became tired of being a fireman, tired of being at the mercy of external events and every nutcase on the planet, and I was sick and tired of being constantly soaked in terror, violence, hatred, and everything else that crushes the human spirit. I needed a new direction, some new sense of meaning and purpose for my life. I had no idea where to turn next, but I knew I had to make a fundamental change.

So one day I up and quit the AP.

Eda, bless her, was very supportive of my decision—she had seen my growing frustrations—but my bosses and colleagues at the AP thought I had gone completely crazy. So did some of my closest friends. Still, soon after leaving the AP, I had three freelance jobs in hand: I was consulting for the news agency Reuters, I was providing some on-air commentary for CNN, and I became a roving correspondent for *The Statesman*, a leading Indian newspaper since the days of Rudyard Kipling. Soon, too, I began something new and very inspiring: teaching the craft of writing. With all of that, I was still taking a pay cut, and I had no benefits and no job security. But I was now happy and free. I had vaulted out the window and was busy chasing squirrels.

One spring day in Paris, a year and a half after I started freelancing, I was having lunch with John Bue, the Paris correspondent of the Voice of America. John was a fine journalist and a fatherly Old World gentleman, with a culture that was half British and half French. We were sharing a couscous and a carafe of red wine at his favorite Moroccan restaurant, and I said to him, "Listen, John. Eda and I really want to take the boys and get away for a while. Might you know of some quiet spot by the Mediterranean Sea?"

John just laughed. "Dear boy, I thought you knew! We have a summer house in Sardinia, right on the beach. Why don't you go there for a month or so?"

"Thanks, John. That sounds marvelous, but money's tight right now and I could never afford a month's rent on a place like that."

"Silly boy," John said. "The place is empty! Hélène and I don't get there until mid-July. Why don't you go, spend a month on the beach, and have the place cleaned, stocked, and ship-shape for our arrival? You'll be doing us a huge favor. In exchange, we can make the rent . . . oh, I don't know. How about $300 for the month? How does that sound?"

How did it sound? Too good to be true! But I still hesitated for a long moment. "Um, John, this is a little delicate, but could we possibly take our dog along? She's very well behaved . . ."

"But of course, dear boy! The place is paradise for a dog!"

And so it began, the next chapter in the adventures of Zelda, the Queen of Paris. Our little street dog from India had conquered Paris and was now off to Italy, Sardinia, and a house by the Mediterranean Sea.

At the outset, I knew next to nothing about the island of Sardinia. With maps and a little research, though, I discovered that Sardinia was the second-largest island in the Mediterranean Sea, after Sicily, and that it was located due south of the island of Corsica, putting it in the heart of the Mediterranean's ancient trade and shipping lanes. The island had a history of settlements going all the way back to Neolithic times, around 6000 BCE, and it had been occupied at various times by the Phoenicians, the Carthaginians, the Romans, the Spanish, and a Germanic tribe called the Vandals. Sardinia was now an autonomous region of Italy, with a strong degree of independence. From what I read, the Sards retained their own distinct dialect, along with a fierce determination to preserve their unique traditions, culture, and cuisine. It sounded great to me. But I also read that an exclusive corner of the island, the Costa Smeralda, attracted the yachting class of Europe and was terribly expensive. So

I called John to express my concern. Was I going to go broke on the island of Sardinia?

John just laughed. "Dear boy, have you ever been to the backwoods of Kentucky or the wild coast of Newfoundland?"

"Uh, no . . ."

"Well, neither have I. But I'm sure that our corner of Sardinia is more like those places than it's like the Costa Smeralda. I can assure you that Sophia Loren will not be sunbathing on our beach, nor will Brigitte Bardot. In fact, apart from a few locals, the beach will be entirely yours."

John then gave me a list of his favorite shops and markets in Muravera, the closest town to his house, and he assured me that his part of Sardinia remained a hidden jewel, rustic yet civilized, and delightfully unspoiled. And affordable, too. Now I couldn't wait to pack up and go.

At the end of the first week in June, everything was ready. Eda and I loaded up the car, belted Justin and Ethan into the backseat, and then in jumped the queen, ready for her month of fun and relaxation beside the Mediterranean Sea. For the royal journey, Eda had prepared a proper throne, with a bag of diving gear bunched on the floor and a comfortable pillow secured on top of that. Perched there, Zelda could stretch out between Justin and Ethan and extend her front legs up onto the console that rested between Eda and me. Nothing, I assure you, was too good for our little girl.

We had a ball on the way down, playing word games with Justin and Ethan, listening to music, and just enjoying the thrill of being out on the open road. On our first day, we meandered down through Burgundy, Lyons, and the valley of the Rhone, and we stopped the first night at a quaint country inn at the foot of the Alps. The place not only accepted dogs, they welcomed Zelda with open arms, both in our room and in their restaurant. The next day we drove through a stretch of the Alps, through the Mont Blanc tunnel, and then down the Mediterranean coast to Genoa, where we were scheduled to board the overnight ferry for Sardinia at 6 p.m. We arrived at the landing in plenty of time and maneuvered our way into the long line of cars parked at the rear of our ship. As we waited to board, we fed Zelda her dinner alongside the car. Then we gave her a last walk to take care of business. Zelda, I must say, was the perfect traveler all the way down. "Well," I said to myself, "so far, so good . . ."

Our ship was not a small ferry boat; it was a big, handsome cruise liner, with several decks and two huge smokestacks rising up alongside the pilot house that commanded the top deck. Across the side of the ship was written *Tirrenia,* the name of the state-run ferry service that made daily runs from Genoa, Livorno, and Rome to several ports along the coast of Sardinia. The shipping line was named after the Tyrrhenian Sea, that part of the Mediterranean off the western coast of Italy, right where we were now about to set sail.

If Eda and I were impressed by the *Tirrenia*, just imagine how big and exciting this ship must have looked through the eyes of Justin, age five, and Ethan, who was all of two and a half. The boys walked up to the ship and I thought both of them would jump straight out of their skin. "Is this *our* boat, Daddy? How many people does it hold? How fast can it go? How many restaurants does it have? Is the food good? Mommy, Daddy, where is Zellie going to sleep?"

The back of the ship was opened out onto the dock like a giant mouth, and when the ship's horn blared, we started our engines and the line of cars filed into the hull. Crew members directed the line of cars around to the front of the boat and there we parked, each car nose to tail. Eda and I gathered up Justin and Ethan, grabbed our overnight bag, put Zelda on her leash, and then we made our way up onto the decks, all in procession, with the queen insisting on being out front. This was another Zelda quirk: She always had to be first. Whether we were walking in the street or in the park, she always had to be out front. What queen, after all, could stand to bring up the rear?

Up on deck, the sea air was bracing and the view was downright spectacular: The evening sun was shining orange and red on the ancient facades of Genoa, giving the city an almost mystical glow. As Eda showed the boys around the deck, I stood at the rail, feeling blessed. In all my working life, I had never before taken a full month off, and spread before us now was nothing but sun, sea, relaxation, great food, and great fun with the boys. At that moment, life seemed just about perfect. Eda was a wonderful travel partner and a fabulous mother, and out on the deck Italian mamas were already cooing over Justin and Ethan, pinching their cheeks and crying, *"Biondo, biondo!"* Blond boy, blond boy! Who, I wondered, could dare ask for anything more?

Then came trouble.

As we pulled out of the harbor, a steward arrived to show us to our cabin, two decks below. To our relief, the cabin was exactly as advertised: roomy and clean, with good beds, fresh linens, and a suitable bathroom. There was also a table to sit at and plenty of room on the floor for us to spread out Zelda's travel blanket, an old tattered quilt that she adored. When I went to tip the steward, he put up his hand: "No dog."

"Che cosa dice, signore?" I asked, thinking a smattering of Italian just might smooth our way.

"I said, *signore*, 'no dog.' No dogs permitted in cabin."

Oh boy. Here we go. "I'm sorry," I said, mustering every drop of civility and politeness I could, "but when I bought the tickets in Paris, they told me there would be no problem bringing the dog."

"*Si, si, signore.* And there is no problem. You can bring the dog—just not in the cabin."

Okay, this was a shakedown. I opened my wallet and pulled out some ungodly sum of Italian lire. But the steward was not impressed. "Follow me, please," he said. "And you bringa de dog."

"Daddy, where are you taking Zelda?"

"Don't worry, boys. It'll be okay."

While Eda stayed with the boys, I followed the steward through the ship and back up to one of the top decks, yanking and pulling Zelda the entire way. She knew something was amiss. We finally stopped beside one of the massive smokestacks. *"Ecco,"* the steward said. Here we are.

I looked at him blankly. At that spot, the roar of the engines was deafening, and the fumes from the smokestacks were even worse. "What do you mean, here we are?"

"Ecco. Cabina per cane." Here. Cabin for dog.

Now he pointed down to a tiny cubicle cut into the side of the ship. It had a miniature door made of iron bars and a latch that bolted from the outside. This was a jail cell, plain and simple. And it was so small that I doubted Zelda could even fit inside. Zelda looked up at me as if to say, "You have *got* to be kidding."

"Okay," I said. "*Tante, tante grazie.* I'll take her back down to the cabin, give her her dinner, and then bring her back up for the night."

The steward just smiled. "*Non penso io.*" No, I don't think so. "You put her here now—or else I take her with me."

The man meant business. "All right then."

I kneeled down, scratched Zelda behind her ears, and did my best to explain the situation. The cage was not down at deck level; it was set up around my thighs, and when I hoisted her up to put her inside, Zelda thrust out her legs and planted them firmly against the outside of the cage. She was *not* getting into that jail cell, come hell or high water. "Sweetie, it's all right," I said. "You just go to sleep and I'll come get you first thing in the morning . . ."

Then I pulled her back and tried to ease her in head first. But Zelda managed to pull free one front leg, and then the other. In an instant she was twisting wildly and spinning out of control. To help, the steward grabbed one of her legs—big mistake! Zelda snarled and lunged out to bite him. And she wasn't just issuing a warning, as she had with the concierge's son. Zelda wanted flesh; she wanted to rip him apart. The steward jumped back, scared out of his wits. I myself was stunned at Zelda's rage; one instant she had been sweet and gentle, the next she was downright murderous. "I am so sorry, *signore,*" I said to the steward. "She's never done that before . . ."

Right away I offered the man that same sum of lire and this time he stuffed it into his pocket and stormed away, swearing to himself and to anyone else who could hear. I was shaken and so was Zelda. I took her to the bow of the ship and found a bench to sit on, hoping the sea air would calm both of us down. But now I faced the great existential question: to tell Eda or not? The issue was not the hush money I had just paid; it was Zelda's rage, her display of outright viciousness. Would this episode scare Eda and get our trip off on entirely the wrong foot? Worse, would Eda now be consumed with worry whenever Zelda was playing around our boys and their pals? Zelda had already created a crisis when she clamped her teeth down on the arm of the concierge's son; another such episode would be a complete disaster. So now I took Zelda by the collar and got right in her face. "I'm furious with you! You put us in a heap of trouble!"

Zelda looked properly sheepish and she nuzzled my hand to beg forgiveness. "Not so fast!" I said. "We still have a major problem here. I don't want to lie to your mother, but I don't want to upset her either. But here's the cold, hard truth: If you ever do that again, if you bite anyone, I will *not* be able to save you. They'll come take you away! And that will be the last we see of you—and the last you see of anyone else. Do you hear me?"

Zelda put her head on my shoes, trying to look as contrite as possible. I left her there for a long time, trying to drive the message home as I figured out what to do next. Finally I rendered my verdict. "Okay, young lady. You're on probation. You had better mind your p's and q's on this trip—or else! Do you understand me? Do you?"

Zelda crawled up into my lap. She understood, all right. "Okay, I am *not* going to tell your mother. This is going to be our secret. Just don't let me down, okay?" With that, Zelda reached up and kissed my face. The deal was sealed and we never said another word about it. And, of course, I took her back to the cabin and the queen spent the night just where she had intended all along, curled up on her quilt, right beside the boys.

The next morning, our ship landed in the north of Sardinia, in the port of Santa Teresa di Gallura. Nearby we found a cafe that had fabulous cappuccinos, hot chocolate for the boys, and a wide assortment of panini, the small Italian sandwiches filled with ham and cheese, egg or tuna salad, or a slice of prosciutto. I immediately felt like I was home again. As much as I loved France, my heart always opened the widest in Italy and around Italians. When I was twenty-three, I had spent a year in Bologna, at the Johns Hopkins School of International Studies, working on my French and Italian and writing my master's thesis, a novel. It was a fabulous year in almost every respect, and it began a love affair with Italy that continues to this very day.

From Santa Teresa, we drove south across the entire island, and we did not dally: We wanted to get to the house in time to swim and get the place ready for the night. As we discovered, Sardinia really has two cultures: the interior, with its rugged mountain terrain and its goats, sheep, and wild boar, and the coastlines, with their beautiful beaches, fishing towns, and seafood bistros. And dotted across the island we saw strange fortresses made of massive, ancient stone. These were called *nuraghis*, and they were used mainly in ancient times as defensive strongholds against foreign invaders. I wondered if those nuraghis said something important about the character and spirit of the Sards themselves.

When we reached the southern tip of the island, we skirted the town of Cagliari, the capital of Sardinia, and then we headed due east along the Mediterranean coast. It was a beautiful drive, through groves of oleander and hills and canyons of limestone and red clay, reminding Eda of her native New Mexico. Outside the town of Muravera, we found our way to a dusty, unpaved road with only a few homes on it, and a mile and a half in we came to John Bue's house. We pulled into the driveway, and we all jumped out of the car and ran up the walkway, Zelda in the lead, of course.

The house and setting were just as John had described. The house stood on a slight embankment, giving it an unfettered view of the Mediterranean Sea. Just below the house was a brick fire pit for barbecuing and just a few steps beyond that was the beach, now shimmering in the heat and empty as far as we could see. The house was built in a simple Mediterranean style, spacious and airy, with white paint and bright blue shutters. The house had a wide terrace facing the beach, perfect for sleeping under the stars, and when we threw open the shutters, every room had a view looking out to the sea. In a few moments, Justin and Ethan had shed their clothes and were running free on the beach, and Zelda was running beside the water, barking happily at the waves. Eda and I looked at each other and right away we knew: Yes, this was it, the closest we would ever come to paradise.

With an easy two days' work, Eda and I had filled the refrigerator, swept out the house, hosed off the terrace, brought in a plumber to fix one of the toilets, hired an electrician to fix some corroded wiring, repaired the barbecue pit, set up a playroom downstairs for Justin and Ethan, and arranged two comfortable beds for Zelda, one on a cot inside and the other out on the terrace, where she could look out to sea in the morning and evening or take a nap in the shade of an olive tree. The Queen of Paris now had her summer palace on the shores of the Mediterranean Sea.

We ate like kings and queens, too. Thanks to the list of shops we had received from John, plus some exploring we did on our own, we had daily picnics on the beach with fresh Italian breads, prosciutto, and salami; a wonderful ewe's milk cheese made on the island; fresh olives, tomatoes, and cucumbers; and figs and blood oranges for dessert and snacks. There was also a wine cooperative in Muravera, and for a few dollars' worth of lire, we could fill bottles or five-gallon jugs with good white, red, or rosé table wine, made right on the island. Dinners? Spaghetti or tagliatelle made fresh that morning, with fresh tomato sauce or a tangy garlic sauce, followed by whatever the boys and I chose to barbecue: a fennel sausage, for instance, or fresh sea bass or mullet bought fresh from the hatchery three hundred yards down the beach. Fruit, gelato, and biscotti for dessert. We were in seventh heaven and so was Zelda, the Gourmet Princess. She developed a special love for fennel sausage, Sardinian cheeses, and the simple, wonderful butter cookies the Italians did so well. Poor girl.

Within a week, we had established a routine: shopping and chores at the crack of dawn, then we'd either go swimming or fly kites on our beach or hop in the car to explore the beaches and coves along the coast. To keep them safe in the water, Eda and I outfitted Justin and Ethan with floaties for their arms, and once they had learned to swim, we bought them fins and masks, so we could go out farther and marvel at the colors of the tropical fish. At the end of the afternoon, we would hurry home to shower, change, and then walk down the road to the Hotel Colostrai, where we reserved a tennis court for every day at 6 p.m. Then, after tennis and dinner, we had a special treat: our nightly races on the beach. "On your marks, get set, go!" and all of us would tear off down the beach. But if I got too far out front, Zelda would run up, grab my pant leg, and send me tumbling. In these races, she wanted either Justin or Ethan to come in first. Noblesse oblige.

One of the best parts of our holiday were the Sards themselves. Through John and Hélène Bue, we linked up right away with the Spignesi family, characters the likes of which you rarely get to meet. The titular head of the family was Angelo Spignesi, a lover of life and tall tales, a lover of wine and fresh pasta, of oysters, clams, and mussels, and, above all, a lover of family, friends, children, dogs, and the sacred Sard and Italian tradition of the glorious Sunday lunch. I called him "The Pascha," for he reigned over those lunches like a sunny Mediterranean potentate.

Pascha provided the wine and the hilarity at our Sunday feasts, but it was his wife, Emilia, who wielded the real power in the family and provided the exquisite Sardinian delicacies. She and Angelo ran a popular kitchen shop in Cagliari, and Emilia was, by anyone's standard, a master chef. While Angelo would start us out with huge platters of oysters, clams, mussels, shrimp, and periwinkles, Emilia would then set before us big bowls of *spaghetti alla bottarga*, a fresh spaghetti in a sauce made from the caviar of fresh mullet, and then would come a sea bass sprinkled with fresh dill, or a rabbit cooked with Roma tomatoes and red wine, or a shoulder of wild boar or goat, simmered for hours with olives, apricots or figs, and fresh herbs and spices. We were usually three generations at the table: Pascha and Emilia; their sons, Franco and Carlo; their daughter, Silvia; her husband, Gianni Sciurru; and their two boys, Marco and Stefano, both close in age to Justin and Ethan. What fabulous times we had. The French fully believe they have perfected what they call *l'art de vivre*, the Art of Living—until they go to Italy or Sardinia and see what they're missing.

In our corner of Sardinia, Zelda quickly became a subject of great fascination. For one thing, very few Americans ever came to Sardinia, especially not to the back country, so the Chutkow family with its two "*biondos*" was already a curiosity. At first, whenever we went to the Farci, our local market and general store in Muravera, or to a local cafe, we would get looks that were at once bewildered and concerned. Who were these Americans? Innocent tourists? Or were they the pilot fish for some new foreign invasion, either of tourists or something more sinister? Either way, as soon as Zelda made her appearance, any and all fears and concerns melted away. The Sards figured that any family traveling with such an exotic beast was probably loony, but certainly not dangerous.

And then there was Zelda on the beach. Whether we went out front to "our beach" or to any of the more isolated coves and beaches around the southern rim of the island, we always arrived like a royal caravan, with the two boys, swimming gear, picnic baskets, towels, and a large, colorful parasol, a form of flag that marked our position and could be seen from a half a mile away. Once we got settled on the sand, Zelda would run down to the water, bark at the waves, maybe take a dip, and when she was good and tired, she would spread herself out under the parasol, enjoying the view and waiting for lunch. On Sundays, when legions of Sards would picnic on the beach in front of our house, kids and parents would come up to our parasol, not to see us, oh no, but to give a little pat to Zelda, who was rapidly becoming the canine queen of our corner of Sardinia.

But even wider fame was still to come.

Having found paradise, Eda and I were not about to let it go; with shameless bribes of lunches and dinners back in Paris, we convinced John and Hélène to let us continue going to their house in Sardinia, year after year. Also, we made ourselves so indispensable in the upkeep and improvement of the house that the Bues eventually stopped charging us any rent at all. We also brought amusement and a degree of notoriety to our corner of Sardinia and to the Spignesi family: I wrote a long piece about life in Sardinia for the Sunday travel section of *The New York Times*. In the piece, Pascha and Emilia held center stage, while Zelda got only passing mention, an omission that I imagine left her royally miffed.

One June a few years later, we again loaded up the car, the boys hopped in the back with their books and music, their Frisbees and diving gear—which now included harpoons for hunting octopus in the shallows—and then Zelda hopped up and wedged in between them. Justin and Ethan were much bigger now, and Zelda had to muscle her way to her throne. We then headed south, and by late morning Eda and I decided to stop in the French countryside for coffee and croissants. Seeing a small cafe up on a hill, we parked the car and got out to stretch our legs. We all needed the break. Then, from out of nowhere, a big German shepherd suddenly came charging down the hill. Before we could stop it, the dog tore right into Zelda, ripping away a huge chunk of her flesh. Zellie shrieked in pain, and for a moment we were all frozen in horror.

This was not an "Ah, dog" moment; this was Crisis Time.

Eda immediately grabbed the boys out of harm's way, while I yelled and chased the German shepherd away. Its owners then came racing down the hill, irate, it seemed, that we had disturbed their sweet, innocent dog. Zelda's wound was nasty. It was a circle six inches across, and the skin was ripped away in a single chunk, leaving the muscle and sinew brutally exposed. We stuffed a cloth into the wound, hoping to stop the bleeding, and then we wound Zelda tightly in beach towels. We demanded the name and address of the nearest vet, and the owners of the cafe gave them to us rather begrudgingly, for reasons we soon came to understand.

Fortunately, the vet was not far away, and in a few minutes he had Zelda sedated and spread across his table. Then he assessed the damage. And the vet was furious. As he explained to us, that German shepherd was a constant danger to the community; it had attacked a man just the week before. In fact, the police had ordered its owners to keep the dog securely chained and inside, pending the outcome of a rabies test. The vet told us his mind was now made up: He would put the dog down later that same afternoon. Zelda would be its last victim.

The vet finished his exam and said to us, *"Elle a de la chance, cette petite."* She's lucky, this little girl. The wound was on the side of her chest, just above the belly. If the German shepherd had gotten her in the neck, a few inches higher, or in the soft part of her belly, a few inches lower, there would have been no way to save her. Zelda would be gone.

As it was, it took the vet almost an hour to clean the wound, shave the area around it, and then stitch her closed. Eda, ever provident, had saved the ripped-away chunk of skin, but there was no way to use it; the vet instead drew her remaining skin together and fixed it securely. Then he wrapped her in bandages, all the way around her trunk, and placed one of those doggie lamp shades around her head, to keep Zelda from tearing at the stitches once the anesthesia wore off. Then he helped us carry our little girl back to the car and lay her gently across the backseat. The man was a prince. "How much do we owe you, kind sir?"

"Pas un sou," the vet said. Not a dime. *"Ces salauds, il vont payer. Et ils vont payer cher."* Those bastards, they will pay. And pay dearly.

Once we were back on the road, the horror of it began to sink in. And Eda and I were both thinking the same thing: How would Justin and Ethan react to it? They had witnessed a brutal attack and seen their beloved "sister" badly wounded and almost killed. Both boys were sitting very quietly now, petting Zelda, making sure she was comfortable, waiting for her to wake up and assure them she was going to be fine. Of course, Eda and I were also consumed by another thought: That German shepherd could just as easily have attacked one of the boys. Then what? The prospect was too awful to even consider.

The next evening we arrived in the port of Genoa, as we had so many times before. When the ship's horn blew, we once again edged our car into the hull of the *Tirrenia*, and soon the five of us were making our way up to the top decks of the ship. This time, though, Zelda was not out front leading the royal procession. Now she was draped in my arms, conscious but wrapped in bandages and still wearing that goofy lampshade around her neck. Now the old Italian mamas on deck paid no attention to our little *biondos*; they saved their cooing for our little Zelda. *"Poverina, ma donna, che cosa è successo?"* The poor girl, oh my God, what has happened?

This time no steward came to hassle us. In fact, several members of the crew sweetly cleared the way as we carried Zelda down to our cabin. By morning, she was the talk of the ship, and as we made our way back to our car, many people came up to express their concern and wish our girl well. Zelda had a way of bringing out the best in just about everyone.

From the port, we headed straight south across the island, and by that same afternoon our heroine was back on her favorite beach, under her parasol, her body still wrapped in bandages and her head still stuffed in the lampshade. We knew that her pain and discomfort were frequently severe, but throughout the days and weeks of recuperation that followed, Zelda never uttered a sound of complaint, she never cursed her fate, she never held a grudge, and she never fell victim to the temptation to feel sorry for herself or to distrust every other dog that came across her path. She may have been born a lowly street mutt, but Zelda possessed the noblest of virtues.

On the following Sunday, and on all the Sundays that followed that summer, Zelda held court under her parasol, enjoying the sea breezes and kissing the hands of the many friends and well-wishers who came to pay their respects and see how she was doing. Emilia Spignesi of course prepared a special stew for Zelda, to speed her recovery, and Angelo, the Pascha, of course spread Zelda's story across the full length and breadth of Sardinia, embellishing it wildly with each and every telling.

With Pascha's gift for the tall tale, the story of Zelda soon grew into a legend, told to children and parents throughout the island, as a stern warning to be careful around dogs we don't know, but also as a shining example of the stoutest of hearts, the richest of character, and the highest forms of grace under pressure. From the lips of Pascha, the Legend of Zelda could never be anything less.

Part Three: California

CHAPTER ELEVEN

Look Homeward, Angel

By the time she was ten, Zelda was a star on three continents.

In her native India, Punjab Singh and our many friends there spread the word of Zelda's adventures, and when she caught the wine burglar, I of course trumpeted the news in a long, humorous piece that I penned for *The Indian Statesman*. I wrote for that paper for fourteen years, and no article I ever did for them generated as much reader fervor and fan mail.

In France and Italy, Zelda's fame continued to grow, thanks to admirers like Pascha and Madame Collin. Now our friends in Paris would no longer call us and ask us to go out for dinner and a movie; they much preferred to invite themselves over for dinner at our place so they could spend a little quality time with Zelda. Likewise, pals of Justin and Ethan would come over not to play with a soccer ball or with Legos; they came over to play with Zelda. It was now commonplace, too, for Marie-Christine Zylberstein to call us with a humble request: She was planning on spending a quiet week out at their country house in Mesnil; would it be all right if she took Zelda along with her for the entire week?

Zelda had yet to set a paw on American soil, but she was already a legend in New York, Boston, New Mexico, and California, thanks to Sheela and to Zelda's many admirers among our American friends and families. One spring, two of Eda's friends from law school in San Francisco came to Paris and took Zelda with them on a trip to Switzerland. With another couple from California, we rented a house on the French Riviera and spent a week on the beach, with Zelda happily in tow. Of course they went back home filled with Zelda stories. Among the Americans in Paris it was the same. With our closest friends in Paris, Joe and Gussy Stanislaw and their three kids, we often spent weekends in Normandy or at their country house south of Paris. And everywhere we went, our little Zelda was always the star of the show.

French vets adored her too, and many had never seen an Indian pi dog before. One time, Eda noticed that Zelda had an uncomfortable layer of plaque that had built up across her back teeth. Nothing being too good for our Zellie, we hunted down a Parisian vet who specialized in dental work and took Zelda in for a cleaning. The chap had an office on the posh Avenue Foch, and walking in was like walking into the lobby of the Hotel Ritz: luxurious carpet, sofa chairs, even a concierge to attend to our every desire and Zelda's every need. Soon Zelda was on the vet's table, happily sedated while the doctor used the latest ultrasound tool to blast away the plaque. We were now worlds away from the humble simplicity of Dr. Karb, her Indian vet—and I had the bill to prove it.

Zelda also had a whole new quartier to explore and conquer. After six years on the rue du Val de Grâce, we had been forced to move. Raymond Aron, our delightful landlord, had come to us with a prickly family dilemma. One of his grandchildren was graduating from college and was eager to have an apartment of her own; could we possibly find another place to live? It was the sweetest possible sort of eviction notice, but we still had to find a new home.

Eda and I wanted to stay on or near the rue du Val de Grâce. This was home, our own special corner of Paris, and it was like a charming French village unto itself. We did not want to leave. But we looked and looked and could find nothing suitable. We then put Madame Collin on the case, hoping that her vast network of contacts might come up with a solution. But she too came up empty.

Then one day I spotted an ad in a French newspaper: "For Sale: Country House in the Middle of Paris." We did not have the means to buy a house in Paris, but the ad was so enticing that I picked up the phone anyway and called the would-be seller.

A vivacious French lady answered the phone, and in rapid-fire French she described her house—and in the most affectionate and glowing terms. The house was big and cheerful and three stories tall, she said, and it was enveloped by gardens and trees. The entire complex was set back from the street, making it into a country haven in the heart of Paris. *"C'est un rêve, Monsieur. C'est un rêve."* It's a dream, Monsieur. It's a dream.

"Well then, Madame," I asked, "why in the world would you want to sell it?"

"Monsieur! I do *not* want to sell it; my husband does! He is retiring, we have another home in the country, and he does not want me to have the burden of the house in Paris. He wants me to be safe and secure, with everything tied up with a pretty bow for the day when he takes leave of this mis-begotten planet!"

"I see . . ." Then I asked, ever so mildly, "Have you considered renting the house? That way you could keep it in the family for your children and grandchildren . . ."

"Rent? Heavens no! This house is a jewel. It needs love. It needs proper care. We can't have renters coming in and making it a mess!"

"Yes, I understand, Madame. Well, let me wish you the best of luck with it . . ."

"Monsieur?"

"*Oui*, Madame?"

"Pardon me for asking, but do I detect just the slightest hint of an American accent?"

I laughed. "*Oui*, Madame. I'm afraid you do . . ."

With that, we started chatting away like long lost friends. Madame Delormeau, it turned out, had had a rather tumultuous time of it in World War II. As a young woman, her parents had shipped her off to Algeria, to protect her from the dangers presented by the Nazi occupation of Paris. She had returned to her beloved city only after it had been liberated and secured by American and Allied forces. "Without the Americans, I ask you, Monsieur Chutkow, what would France be today?"

"I don't know, Madame."

"Well, I do know: We'd be Germany!"

We chatted awhile longer and then Madame Delormeau said, "You know, Monsieur, you really should see my house. Maybe there is something we can do . . ."

Eda and I did go see the house and right away we fell in love with it. Then, somehow, Madame Delormeau convinced her husband, a doctor who for decades had run his practice right there in the house, that we would be ideal renters and that renting to us would allow their jewel of a home to remain in their family for generations to come. It also helped, I'm sure, that Madame Delormeau had a dog she was crazy about, a dog who got along famously with our little Zelda.

Yes, our luck was holding.

Indeed, the new house had a touch of magic. It was located farther south on the Left Bank, at 202 Avenue du Maine, a busy, noisy boulevard running out to the edge of the city. The house itself, though, was set back inside a private courtyard, and when we closed the doors to the street, the courtyard was quiet and serene; to us it felt like an island sanctuary in the heart of Paris. There were four houses inside our complex, each enclosed by an elegant iron fence and each surrounded by flowers and trees. Our house had a stately feel and was painted white with gray shutters and trim. We had a small terrace out back, perfect for eating outside in the spring and summer, and in the front of the house we had a small garden with a lovely cherry tree that stood in the middle. In summer, Zelda would sleep in the shade of that tree, and in spring it would again burst into bloom, and then for months afterward it would spread its pink and white petals across the lawn and right up the steps of our front stoop.

In the middle of the courtyard there was a long, narrow walkway, and Justin, Ethan, and I turned it into our own private field of dreams. There, Justin and I would play catch with a baseball or football, Ethan would ride his bike there with Emily, his pal from next door, and Zelda, the lucky dog, would stretch out in the sun or happily rub noses with *Réglisse*, Licorice, the neighborhood boxer who frequently wandered in, eager to play.

Heaven.

We all settled in nicely on the Avenue du Maine. Eda, ever the Wonder Mom, was now practicing law with an international firm with offices on the Champs-Elysées, and Justin and Ethan were growing up as bilingual and bicultural kids. At home, they spoke American English, listened to Elvis Presley and Bob Dylan, and ate hamburgers, steaks, and apple pie, while in Parisian homes they listened to Jacques Brel and ate oysters, lentils, escargot, and *tarte tatin*. Monday through

Saturday morning the boys went to a public school around the corner, and every day they would come home speaking French like Parisian truck drivers and singing filthy little tunes they had picked up in the schoolyard.

Zelda was enjoying life too. She had her yard to play in, a charming sunroom upstairs to nap in, a whole new neighborhood to explore, and now she added a new delicacy to her over-indulged gourmet palate: white truffles, fresh from Italy. You see, going to or from Sardinia, we often stopped off in Florence to see some old family friends of mine: Umberto and Giovanna Balatresi and their children, Rebecca and Tiberio. The Balatresis ran a gift shop and art gallery a few steps from the Ponte Vecchio, but Umberto was now spending every free moment out in the countryside hunting truffles. He was like a man reborn, and Umberto loved to share with us some of his treasures. Zelda, alas, did not have the training or the temperament to hunt truffles, but she loved to smell them and taste them. We all did, especially grated over Giovanna's fresh pasta or scrambled eggs.

Zelda also had regular visits from her soul buddy, Sheela. Almost every winter, Sheela would visit us on her way to or from Gstaad. By this time, Sheela had become something of a legend in her own right. She kept house and cooked for the Galbraith family, and she was famous in the Harvard community for her banana breads, her Indian delicacies, and her wonderful spirit. As we had hoped, the Galbraiths treated Sheela like a member of their family, and with their help she had become a U.S. citizen and had also brought her son, Tony, and his family to America.

Sheela always arrived in Paris with amusing stories about her new life in America. As she often told us, Sheela frequently cooked Indian delicacies for Julia Child, their neighbor in Cambridge, and she often prepared elaborate dinners for family friends such as Angie Dickinson and the Kennedy kids. As we heard from Sheela, Jackie Kennedy was also a frequent guest of the Galbraiths, and Sheela liked her immensely. "Very, very nice woman," Sheela told us. "Very kind. Very modest." According to Sheela, she and Jackie often had long, intimate chats, and Zelda, the luckiest dog in the world, was a frequent topic of their conversations.

One year I picked Sheela up at the airport, and driving back into Paris I asked her what was new and exciting in her life. Mrs. Galbraith, she told me, was sending her to cooking school. *French* cooking school. "Wow," I said. "That's wonderful! Is French cooking difficult to master?"

"Nah," Sheela said. "It's easy. You just add liquor to every dish and give it a fancy name." That was Sheela, pure as snow.

Sheela remained, in every respect, a cherished member of our family. She loved her buddy "Jelda," and she absolutely adored Justin and Ethan. She cooked for them, fussed over them, and always brought them little gifts from America. She was their beloved Indian grandma. She also liked our new house, and she often went out to poke around the neighborhood. Sheela wasn't going out shopping or looking for a cafe; she was looking for a church to attend on Sunday morning. Catholic, Protestant, Buddhist, it didn't matter to Sheela; she would find God wherever she went.

Seeing Sheela always made me miss Punjab Singh and Dhobi Dubinksy. Via Myron, I heard that Gene Kramer, his replacement as the AP bureau chief in New Delhi, had fired the dhobi for some minuscule offense, and that news caused me great pain. Punjab, I knew, was still going strong. I had sent him a postcard at the Jor Bagh taxi stand, and to my delight he had sent me a card in return, with a blue and gold painting of the Hindu god Krishna on the front. In Paris, I often thought of what Punjab had said the morning Justin was born: From that moment on, everything would change, and nothing would be more important than that child and the ones who would follow. How right he was.

Eda and I both had exciting careers, but in line with Punjab's admonition our first priority was always to be conscientious parents. Like most of the parents we knew in Paris, we were strict about homework, strict about good manners at the table, strict about limiting the boys' TV time, and insistent that Justin and Ethan treat their teachers and elders with proper respect. On top of that, Eda diligently fed the boys a steady diet of Paris culture, from concerts, museums, and galleries to piano lessons, swimming lessons, riding lessons, and puppet shows in the Luxembourg Gardens. At night, before bed, it was my turn. I would curl up with my guys and we would read the Babar stories or St. Exupery's *The Little Prince* or the marvelous whimsies of William Steig, books like *Farmer Palmer's Wagon* and *The Amazing Bone*. We were Americans in Paris, and we felt it was both our privilege and our obligation to stuff our boys to the gills with everything Paris had to offer by way of art, music, language, and literature—whether they liked it or not. Who knew, after all, which tiny seed might one day take root and come full flower?

One Saturday morning at a nearby flea market, Eda and I found an old French school desk that we simply had to have for Justin and Ethan. It was a desk made for two, and it was crafted in a dark mahogany that was now scarred and burnished with age. The desk had two holes in the upper corners for inkwells, and the large work surface sloped down like a drafting table. Under the top, the desk had two spacious cubby holes, and Eda always kept them filled with crayons, watercolors, brushes, colored pencils, and reams of paper. The desk came with a matching stiff-backed bench for two, itself a testament to the upright posture and discipline that French teachers demand from their pupils. The desk, of course, was an emblem of our highest parental ambitions: We hoped that one day Justin or Ethan would be sitting there, drawing, painting, or writing, and some magical light would come on—and a great artist or writer or teacher soon would be born.

Yes, in Paris we had at our fingertips every conceivable tool a parent could dream of, every tool, that is, except the best one: Baseball.

Like many Americans, I grew up with baseball coursing through my veins. Later, living in India and Paris, I followed the game from afar, and I kept my eye on the ups and downs of my favorite team, the San Francisco Giants. As Justin and Ethan got older, though, my heart really began to ache. I wanted to take my boys to a ball game, I wanted them to feel the excitement of a big league park, and I wanted them to have the joys and life lessons that only baseball can deliver. Yes, our life in Paris was almost perfect, but every spring I felt there was something missing, something absolutely essential that I wanted Justin and Ethan to have. I wanted them to hear the crack of the bat, I wanted them to smell the freshly mown grass, I wanted them to feel the rising pump of your heart when you and your pals are leading going into the ninth, and I wanted them to know, deep down inside, the soaring, delicious, incomparable rush that you feel in your heart and even your soul when that final, game-winning out lands with a satisfying *thunk*! in the leather pocket of your very own glove.

Yes, I wanted all that for Justin and Ethan, and so profound was the feeling that one day I sat down and wrote an article titled "Fathering without Baseball." In it, I tried to draw together the many things that baseball teaches us, without even trying to: Tradition. Character. Courage. Commitment. Fair play. Passion. Pride. Discipline. Teamwork. Community spirit. And, perhaps above all else, the uncompromising Quest for Excellence. Yes, all those values and virtues come through baseball, and I wanted my boys to understand all that, and I wanted them to understand just how deeply baseball is woven into the fabric of the American spirit and the American Dream.

For a long time, Eda and I struggled with the idea of leaving Paris. Life was awfully good in Europe; why go back? And where would we go? New York? San Francisco? Washington, D.C.? None of those places won our unanimous favor.

Then one day I was in San Francisco doing a story for *The New York Times*, and I had dinner with Eda's longtime friend Susie Tompkins. With her business partner of the time, Jane Tise, Susie had created the fashion empire Esprit, and "by chance"—Mother Teresa would chuckle at that—Susie and Jane had been on the same Air France flight that first took me to India. The following night in New Delhi, around midnight, Susie and Jane just "happened" to be in the dining room of the Ashoka Hotel when I came back from my first day on the job. With them was an attractive young woman named Eda Cole. We all had dinner together that night, and as I was leaving, Susie took me aside: "Take care of Eda, will you? She's a wonderful woman." Yes, ma'am! Soon Eda and I were married, and soon Susie became the unofficial godmother to Justin and Ethan. Now, over dinner, Susie asked me to do her a favor.

"Paul, I'm thinking about buying a piece of property in the Napa Valley, a place sitting high above the Silverado Trail. I'm not sure about it, though. Would you go have a look and tell me what you think?"

The next morning I made my first trip to California Wine Country. From San Francisco I drove north across the Golden Gate Bridge, the morning sun shining on its russet-colored towers and guide wires, and then I made my way up to Sonoma County and the village of Glen Ellen. I wanted to see Wolf House, the place Jack London had built toward the end of his tumultuous life. Behind his house and the tiny museum beside it, there was a small lake—a perfect spot for walks with Zelda. Then I climbed up a hill to a serene, tree-shaded mound looking out across the Valley of the Moon. Jack London is buried there, and I could not imagine a finer place to contemplate life or to rest eternally in peace.

From there I drove up over the Mayacamas Mountains and down into the Napa Valley. It was May, the air was warm, and the leaves on the vines were already a brilliant green. Hungry, I stopped for lunch at a place I happened to see alongside the road, the Bistro Don Giovanni. On the menu that day was a hearty dish straight from the hills of Sardinia: penne pasta with fresh mushrooms and wild boar. Perfect! And my first thought was, "Bring me a doggie bag; Zelda would love a taste of this boar!"

After lunch, I drove a short ways east and then turned north onto the Silverado Trail. Just beyond Trancas Avenue, the town of Napa slipped away and the landscape opened out onto acre upon acre of glorious vineyard. As far as the eye could see, rows of precision-planted vines marched in stately procession across the valley floor and straight up the slopes on either side. Right away I could feel my spirit soar. In America, there are other drives that I find exciting, but for raw beauty I had found very few that could compare to the Silverado Trail. To me, this was it: big sky, big landscapes, a perfect place to dream big dreams. And what a perfect place for a writer like me.

Inspired, the following Christmas I brought Eda and the boys back with me to California Wine Country. Now we were unanimous: This was it. This was the place to settle in America. And so began the final chapters in Zelda's magical odyssey. The Indian Slum Dog, the Gourmet Princess, and the Queen of Paris was now ready for her last hurrah: Zelda was coming to America, to the hills and vineyards of Sonoma County and the Napa Valley. Yes, Zelda had to be the luckiest dog in the world.

CHAPTER TWELVE

All Good Things

It was not easy to leave Paris.

Eda and I had thrived there, Justin and Ethan had grown up there, and over the course of our twelve years in Paris each of us had developed unbreakable bonds to friends and places and to the special spirit that Paris holds and nurtures. And Zelda, of course, thought that Paris and Sardinia were paradise on Earth.

Still, in the summer of 1989 we knew it was time to leave. So we packed up our belongings, got everything set, and drove down to Italy to spend one last month swimming, eating, and reveling on the beaches of Sardinia. Then we said our good-byes to Paris and to a time in our lives that we knew could never be matched.

This time, Zelda got to fly with us. At Charles de Gaulle Airport, we all stood at the gate, watching through the window as Zelda's traveling crate rolled up the ramp and disappeared into the cargo bay of the big 747. The sight of her in that moment remains indelibly printed on my mind. She was up on all fours and leaning forward, her head held high and proud. She was the picture of courage and dignity, ready for the next phase of her storied life, come what may.

We had an easy, eleven-hour flight, and when we landed in San Francisco, we found Zelda looking happy and relaxed, as if she had slept the entire way. At the airport we all piled into a rental car, and soon were headed north across the Golden Gate Bridge—and to brand-new lives in America. Zelda, of course, resumed her usual throne between Justin and Ethan in the backseat, with her long, elegant front legs reaching up onto the console between Eda and me. What a gal. And how far she'd come. The little imp from the streets of New Delhi was a well-mannered lady now, almost fourteen, her muzzle and eyebrows growing a bit gray. As I drove, once or twice she reached up and gave me a little kiss on the cheek. On one of my trips to Africa, a shaman had read my fortune in the sand

and said that I was a lucky man: I would have two sons and a daughter. When I later told Eda about it, she said, "Well, that's Zelda, of course . . ." Yes, that was Zelda. My daughter, my Indian wife, and now my constant sidekick and pal.

As we drove north, I turned on the car radio and there they were: my San Francisco Giants. They were playing the Chicago Cubs, as I recall, and right there in the car our boys got their first taste of Major League Baseball. Justin had just turned twelve, Ethan was now nine, and although they had never seen or heard a big league ball game before, they immediately felt the excitement coming through the radio. Within minutes, our boys had a whole new pantheon of heroes to admire and follow: Will "The Thrill" Clark, Matt Williams, Kevin Mitchell, Steve "Bedrock" Bedrossian, the Giants' closer. The KNBR broadcasters and color team also worked in some Giants lore, featuring Willie Mays, Willie McCovey, and Juan Marichal. Within an hour both boys were hooked; such is the power and mystique of America's game.

Eda and I looked at housing, schools, and job opportunities in several corners of California Wine Country, and we finally found a welcoming spot amid the hills and vineyards of Sonoma County. It was a low-slung ranch house in an area called Rincon Valley. For the boys, it was an easy bike ride to public schools. For Eda and me it was a rich taste of country life, but still close enough to Santa Rosa, the county seat and a good place for Eda to practice law. This was also a very comfortable spot for me to base myself as a freelance writer. Sonoma had emerged as a vibrant hub of wine and food, and the Napa Valley was just a short drive away. I planned to write about food and wine and many of California's leading pioneers in business and culture.

And Zelda?

Well, it took Zelda about two hours—and a half of her first cheeseburger—to feel happy and settled in America. Our new house was bordered by a big pasture with horses in the back, and our yard had plenty of room for Zelda to roam free, chase squirrels, and stretch out in the sun. And close by were wonderful lakes and parks, perfect for family picnics or for the kind of hikes that Zelda and I enjoyed together.

Food-wise, too, the Gourmet Princess was not about to suffer. That summer we did a lot of barbecuing on the patio behind our house, under the limbs of the giant redwood that rose serenely above our heads. Steak, fresh salmon, spare ribs, corn on the cob, big country salads—we melded good American cooking with the spirit of Paris and Sardinia, and celebrated them all right at our table. Eda, ever resourceful, crafted for us our own redwood picnic table and lounge chairs; there was nothing this woman was unable to do. And at night, after dinner, we often tuned in to the Giants on the radio or TV. Even Zelda seemed to enjoy the games.

It was exciting being back in America, reconnecting with friends and family and that good old American can-do spirit, but by the start of October I was getting worried about our little Zelda. She was awfully gray around the muzzle now, and instead of poking her nose into every corner of the yard, she now spent long hours stretched out on her pad, sleeping in the sun. I spent my mornings and early afternoons at the keyboard, and by 2 p.m. I always needed a break and a brisk walk. But Zelda was harder to rouse now, and she didn't seem very happy if our walks went on too long. Something was up; at first I thought it was simply old age.

Then things took a mysterious turn.

One morning, we all woke up bursting with excitement: Today was Game One of the World Series, and our San Francisco Giants were going for the crown. I had been a Giants fan since the age of seven, but in the span of my life the Giants only once had gone to the World Series and come out the champs. Could this be the year they would do it again? Justin, Ethan, and I could only hope and cheer and follow every pitch. Eda was not a fanatic about baseball, not the way we were, but she was a good sport and gamely put up with our zany passions and baseball superstitions.

Zelda was another matter. On that morning of Game One, when the Giants would face the Oakland A's, Zelda was nervous and all out of sorts. She spent the day camped under my desk, coiled in a tight little ball. When I laid down beside her, I could feel her shaking with fear. Right away I took her temperature, inspected her gums, and inspected her body for any unusual bumps or lesions. I'm no vet, but I could find no sign of physical trouble or even discomfort. Could our Zellie possibly be worrying about the fate of our Giants? As soon as I thought it, I slapped myself, mentally, across the kisser. "Come on, lad! Sure, she's intuitive, but a dog worrying about the Giants? Have you lost your freaking mind?"

Still, as the first pitch drew near, Zelda got worse. I did my writing at a big table set against the wall, and Zelda stayed constantly under my feet, pressed tightly into the corner formed by the wall and the base of the desk. That was like her private tent or shelter. On other days, if I went out to the kitchen for a glass of water or a cup of coffee, Zelda would always trot along behind me. No longer. Now she stayed curled up inside her shelter. Well, maybe she's just tired out, I thought, and left it at that.

The Giants lost Game One. Playing on their home field in Oakland, the A's shut them out 5–0. Justin, Ethan, and I listened to every pitch, and I can tell you there was no joy in Mudville that night. In Game Two, the A's whipped us again, this time by a score of 5–1. Now we all slid into the foulest of moods. Still, as we approached Game Three, I put on my best game face and told the guys, "Don't worry. When the going gets tough, the tough get going." Secretly, though, my hopes were sinking. And I was getting increasingly worried about Zelda. Nothing could snap her out of her funk.

On the morning of the crucial Game Three, I made breakfast for Justin and Ethan with all the exuberance and baseball voodoo that I could muster. "Today we win, guys," I chirped. "We're back on our own turf at Candlestick Park. And besides, today is October 17th, my sister Jil's birthday. How can we possibly lose?"

To set an uplifting tone for the day, I prepared a sumptuous breakfast: fried eggs, bacon, English muffins, and coffee for Eda and me. I was hoping that Zelda would smell that bacon and come join us for breakfast. But no. She stayed huddled under my desk. I called softly for her to come, but she wouldn't budge. Okay, I thought: That's it. If she's not better by the end of the day, I'll take her to the vet.

All morning long I worked on a story for *The Indian States-man*, and by noon I needed a break. So I roused Zelda and we went for walk down the quiet country road in front of our house. When we got about fifty yards down the road, though, Zelda abruptly turned around and hurried home. I called her to come back, but she refused. Then I whistled and shouted, but her mind was made up: no walk today. And as soon as I opened the door for her, she rushed right back to her shelter beneath my desk. Now I started to get really worried: This was not at all like our little Zelda.

After so many years in journalism, I prided myself on being able to write a decent story in any place, fair or foul, and at any time of the day or night. But now I felt all out of sorts, consumed first and foremost by Zelda's mysterious state, and the story I was writing simply refused to flow. I fought it to a draw, though, and wrapped it up at 4:30 p.m. Justin and Ethan were due home shortly, in time for the first pitch of Game Three, set for about 5:05. On most days, I would have sent the dispatch by fax right from the house, but our fax machine was broken, so I had to take the copy to a local pack-and-ship place and use their fax. This was before the Internet era, so I could not yet file my stories to India electronically.

"Come on, Zellie!" I called. "Let's go for a ride in the car!"

She wouldn't budge.

"Come on, Sweetheart. A little air will do you good!"

No way. She refused to move from under my desk. So I got in the car and drove over to Pak Mail. I arrived at a few minutes to five, and the owner, my buddy Chuck, was his usual cheerful self. We stood at his counter awhile, schmoozing, and then Chuck took my dispatch and slid it into his fax machine. The call connected, and just as my story rolled into the fax, bound for Calcutta, the counter I was leaning on suddenly jolted downward, almost tumbling me to the ground. What the . . . ? I looked out in the parking lot and there was my car, a good-size Nissan, pitching back and forth like a toddler's rocking horse.

Earthquake!

I raced home, worrying about Eda at work and imagining Justin, Ethan, and Zelda pinned at home under a pile of rubble. When I got there, though, the house was intact and the boys were shaken but okay. Eda called to say she was okay too. This was my first earthquake, and it was scary indeed. Justin and Ethan were not as upset as I was. As they told me, they had gone through earthquake drills at school, so they knew exactly what to expect. Welcome to California.

Zelda was a whole other story. When I got home, she was still curled up under my desk and shaking like an outboard motor. When I knelt down to get her, she jumped into my arms, yelping and snuffling. "Oh, Sweetheart," I said, stroking her. "Just like a little baby . . ."

Then we turned on the TV and began to see pictures of the destruction. This was the big one, the Loma Prieta earthquake, and it registered between 6.9 and 7.1 on the Richter Scale. Via TV, we soon got glimpses of the breadth of devastation: Homes, buildings, highways, and entire neighborhoods were leveled in San Francisco and in other parts of Northern California. In all, 63 people were killed in the quake, another 3,750 were injured, and some 12,000 people were left homeless. Even more were left traumatized. This was the worst quake in San Francisco since 1906.

And our Zelda had felt it coming.

We realized that a short time later, when one of the TV newscasters explained that some dogs have a strange sixth sense that enables them to detect tectonic shifts and an imminent earthquake. This was a revelation; who knew that some dogs had that power? Not us. So now I understood why Zelda had been acting so strangely these past few days. And when she continued to tremble in my arms, I knew that some aftershocks were sure to follow. I turned to Justin and Ethan: "Tell me, guys, what did they teach you to do in your earthquake training?"

"Duck under desks and tables, and get as close as you can to walls and door frames." So that was it. Zelda had instinctively known what to do in a quake: hide under the desk and stay close to the wall. What a girl. Heck, she could have written the emergency handbook. "Zellie," I said to her, "you are one extraordinary being!"

One of the scariest things we saw on TV was Candlestick Park, filled with sixty thousand fans getting ready for Game Three. The quake sent a rolling shock through the stadium—and the beginning of a rolling panic too, especially as the huge light towers swayed chaotically, looking as if they were ready to fall. It could have been horrific. But then the shock waves subsided, the light towers stabilized, and most of the people inside the park regained their composure. As it was, the old stadium came through with only minor damage. Eda, Justin, Ethan, and I watched the scene at Candlestick with our hearts in our throats.

The powers that be in Major League Baseball wisely put the World Series on hold for ten days. When Game Three finally was played, the A's beat our Giants handily, and they took the next one too, to make it a four-game sweep and win the crown. But you know what? By then, none of us really cared. The earthquake had brought us a stark lesson about what was most important in life, and now we were much more concerned with the people who had been killed or wounded or who had lost their homes. As we saw up close, the earthquake was a monstrous act of nature, and its wrath was both indiscriminate and pitiless, striking rich and poor, saint and sinner with equal blindness and equal vengeance. We got the message loud and clear: Live life to the fullest, love to the fullest; you never know what tomorrow will bring.

Within a few days, Zelda was back to her sprightly self, playing with the boys and going with me on hikes in the hills of Sonoma County. The tremors had subsided, and Zelda was recovering nicely. Now, though, I saw this little dog in a whole new light. If she had inside her the power to sense an earthquake coming, and sense it days in advance, what other powers might she possess? I began observing Zelda much more closely, and I was even more astonished by this strange little beast.

When the boys were little, Zelda had treated them both about the same—at least I didn't notice much difference—but as they got older and began to take on distinct personalities, Zelda seemed to understand and react accordingly. Justin, for instance, loved his new school in America. After his very first day, he came home from school with stars in his eyes. "So," I asked him, "how was it?"

"Wow!" he said. "Amazing!"

"Really? Why?"

"The teacher asked me what I thought!"

For Justin, this was something new and exciting. In his schools in Paris, the teachers taught in the classic French manner: learning by rote. The teacher would give the lesson, and the students would take in as much as they could. Then at test time the students were expected to regurgitate exactly what they had heard from the teacher. The style at Justin's Rincon Valley Junior High was much freer, more engaging, and more stimulating, and Justin drank it in, eager to succeed. He studied ferociously, he played soccer ferociously, and he worked just as hard to pick up the skills of baseball. His ambition and will to win were admirable, but they made his life a pressure cooker—and Zelda, instinctively, knew just what to do. If Justin was going at the books too hard, Zelda would sense it and arrive with a tennis ball, eager to play. At night, when he needed to let go, she would climb up onto his bed and curl in next to him, ready for a soothing scratch or a relaxing sleep right alongside him.

With Ethan, Zelda had a very different style. Ethan, Mr. I Decide What I Eat, was more outgoing and social than Justin, and he always had a posse of friends around to keep him relaxed and amused. Even at a young age, Ethan was a creative kid, with a special fondness and talent for music, something he inherited from his mother's side. School? That was another matter. At our first parent-teacher night in America, Eda and I sat down with Ethan's teacher. "Well," he said, "things are going . . . well, okay. Ethan's a dreamer, of course, and, as you know, he's a little slow . . ."

Eda and I looked at each other. A little slow? Ethan? The kid spoke, read, rhymed, and punned in two languages, he played the piano well, and he knew forty or fifty Elvis songs by heart and two dozen Beatles' hits as well. So we asked his teacher, "Why do you think he's a little slow?"

"Well, he speaks English with a funny accent, and in math he has trouble with long division."

Eda and I just laughed. The teacher hadn't done his homework. He had no clue that Ethan had spent his first nine years in Paris, going to school only in French, and as for long division, well, French kids learn to do it in an entirely different format. No wonder Ethan appeared to be slow and struggling. Still, all of this made school, at the outset, frustrating for Ethan, and at home in his room, doing his homework, he would get fidgety and sometimes upset. Then Zelda would arrive for some of their usual jousting and wrestling, perfect for Ethan to blow off some steam. Thanks to Zelda, Ethan could then sit back down and master the task at hand. I was amazed at our girl. With Justin, she was a soulmate. With Ethan, she was a playmate. Just imagine the intelligence and sensitivity that resided inside her.

And how was Zelda with me?

Ah, Zelda and I. Eda and Zelda were like mother and daughter: Eda loved her from the depths of her heart, but she was also the strict mother, and sometimes the two of them had fierce battles of will. As we saw with the Battle of Paris and the resulting hunger strike, Eda quickly became annoyed if, in her eyes, Zelda was acting too regal or was being overindulged. And I just made matters worse. Zelda had a passion for pizza crusts, whatever was left after the rest of us had chomped out the middle. Whenever we had pizza at home, Zelda would sit right next to my chair, drooling onto my pant leg or down onto my shoes. "Zelda, go away, now!" I would bark, in my sternest voice, but as soon as Eda looked away, I'd slip Zellie another crust. It was wrong, of course, but the devil inside me could never resist.

The point is, Zelda and I had a special understanding. Because I had my office at home, Zelda and I spent an enormous amount of time alone together. In fact, for days at a time we would spend nearly every minute together. When I got up, she got up. When I went into the shower, Zelda would sit on the bathmat, waiting for me to come out. When I went into the kitchen to make coffee and breakfast, Zelda would be right there too. When I went to the market—if it wasn't too hot—Zelda would ride along with me, and when I drove over the Mayacamas Mountains to the Napa Valley to work on a story, I loved to take Zelda along with me, as my companion and copilot. Like me, she loved to see the landscapes and beauty of the Silverado Trail.

By now, we were almost inseparable. When we went for a ride in the car, I would open the back door for Zelda, but as soon as she hopped in, she would go up to the front and install herself in the passenger seat. For Zelda there was no more riding in the back—unless Eda was in the car. In Zelda's mind, her place was up front, right beside me. There she would sit quietly, watching the road, keeping me company, always alert for danger. As Sheela had told us, Zelda saw herself as my Indian wife, and there was certainly truth in that. But I think she also saw herself as our guardian angel, not just for me but for all of us. That pure and noble calling was inside her too.

This was entirely new for me. The dogs we had when I was growing up were pals of mine, yes, but Zelda and I shared an intimacy that was on a whole other level. With her exquisite radar, Zelda was acutely attuned to me, and I to her. She not only understood me, oftentimes I thought she could actually read what I was thinking and feeling at any given moment. Zelda gave me comfort, she gave me joy, and if she wanted a humble pizza crust, by golly she'd have it.

One day, out for a walk in front of our house, Zelda seemed to catch her right front paw on a stone or rock. The paw flopped back, Zelda cried out, and the paw just sort of hung there, as if the ligaments had been torn or badly sprained. But the ligaments seemed okay to me; I figured Zelda was just pooped. From there she bravely soldiered on, without a complaint, but I could see that one of her paws kept flopping down and scraping against the pavement. I took her home and called the vet.

Zelda by now had turned fourteen, her whiskers and eyebrows were white with age, and I felt an odd heaviness and resignation coming from her when I hoisted her up onto the examination table. Feeling around her tummy, the vet found an unusual mass. Yes, cancer. The lump was still small, but the vet said it could be sapping her energy and making her weak. "Should we operate?" I asked. "We could," the vet said. "But she's old now, and it would cause her a lot of discomfort, and it would probably extend her life for only an extra month or two. In any case, she's a hearty girl, and I think she still has several good months in front of her."

Several months.

Now life became complicated and a bit schizophrenic. A part of me was living a quiet life in California Wine Country; another part of me still held the fire of the foreign correspondent: When history was being made, I wanted to be there to see it, feel it, and write about it. Back in August of 1980, when Lech Walesa and his fellow members of Poland's Solidarity trade union went on strike and took control of the shipyards in Gdansk, I wanted to be there. And when Polish authorities refused to grant me a visa, the AP sent me to Bonn, Germany, to anchor the coverage and edit the raw copy coming in from Gdansk. That was the first breach in the wall of the Soviet Empire. Now, in November 1989, the Berlin Wall itself started to crack, and again I wanted to be there, to see that noxious symbol of the Cold War come crashing down. I wanted to see the Soviets finally forced to open their doors and set people free. So I wangled a magazine assignment to Berlin, and there I got to see it firsthand: the fall of the empire and the inspiring triumph of liberty, so reminiscent to me of Mrs. Gandhi's fall twelve years before.

Being in Berlin was exhilarating, but when I got back home and saw Zelda, I was shocked to see her state of decline. Now our girl had very little energy, in fact far too little to even go out on a hike. She spent most of her time sleeping on her mat in the driveway or curled up at my feet. Zelda had been on digitalis for years—our vet in France had detected an irregular heart beat—and now our local vet upped her dosage, thinking it might give her energy a boost. It didn't. And then and there my spirits began to sink.

Eda, bless her, went back to cooking special meals for Zelda, and we and the boys did everything we could to keep Zellie cheerful and smiling. One afternoon, though, when Zelda and I were alone in the house, we had lunch together, and then I went back to the bedroom to take a nap. Zelda followed me and jumped up on the bed, and I didn't have the heart to shoo her down. A half an hour later, I was sound asleep when there came this horrible sound. I awoke to find Zellie doubled over in pain and vomiting on our bedspread. Now I knew we had reached decision time.

I cleaned up Zellie, then tossed our bedspread into a big trash bag and took it to the cleaners. When I got back, I took Zelda and sat her down beside me. "We have to talk," I said to her. "I don't want to tell your mother about that bedspread. That has to be between you and me, okay?"

I felt sure that Zelda was agreeing.

"But we have some decisions to make. That lump in your tummy has gotten awfully big. And it bothers you, doesn't it?"

Zelda now put her head in my lap.

"The doctor says we can operate. And down the road it might make you feel better. But it's going to hurt. And it might not help you very much. You need to tell me what you want to do . . ."

I listened as intently as I could, but I could hear no answer. And I could see no sign that she was understanding. A few days later, though, Zelda abruptly stopped eating. We offered her the meals she loved most: steak and chicken, hamburger and salmon, even pizza crusts. She would sniff, take a nibble or two, and that would be that. I knew she was telling me, as eloquently she could, that she wanted no operation, no force-feeding, no more digitalis, and no heroic measures of any sort. She had lived a full and joyous life, and she was now ready to go. Yes, this humble little street dog, our guardian angel, was teaching us lessons right to the end, lessons about dignity and acceptance, about courage and grace.

We waited a few days, to enjoy her presence and see if she might change her mind, and when she didn't, Eda and I decided that the proper thing to do was to hold a family ceremony. We cooked a special dinner, lit candles, opened a bottle of wine, and sat on the floor in a circle around Zelda, eating with plates in our laps and sharing Zelda stories. I recalled our first romps in the park back in Jor Bagh, with the little imp nipping me on the bottom. Eda recalled her famous battle of wills over the dog food in Paris, and Justin and Ethan reminded us of her love-ins with Sheela and of our nightly races on the beach in Sardinia, when Zelda would grab my pant leg to make sure that Justin or Ethan would win the race. Of course too, we all remembered Zelda and the terrible earthquake of the year before.

After dinner, we brought out our sleeping bags and gathered close to Zelda, and all through the night Justin and Ethan stroked her and comforted her and put their heads down right next to hers. Zelda lay on her side, breathing quietly, licking our hands, absorbing our love. This was a sad and yet beautiful passage, and when dawn came I knew in my heart that for the length of our lives and wherever we went, Eda, Justin, Ethan, and I would always carry her special spirit safely inside us.

In the morning, after everyone else had said their good-byes and left the house, I held Zelda for a long time in my arms, hugging her, kissing her, and thanking her for all the adventures, humor, and wisdom she had brought into our lives. Fourteen years is a very long time, and throughout those years she gave us everything she had inside her. She held nothing back, her emotions were pure, and she asked so little of us in return. How many among us have done as much?

Finally, when her breathing began to falter, I carried Zelda out to the car and laid her down gently on the seat beside me. We drove to the vet, and before going in we sat together for a long time, silently, with her head in my lap. Then I gave her a final kiss, a last scratch on her ears, and said my good bye. Zelda's magical odyssey—and the best part of ours—had come to a close.

Acknowledgments

Zelda and I did not write this book alone. We had the generous support of an exceptional group of people, and we want to salute each of them right here

First, we want to thank Sheela Karintikal, our beloved cook, nanny, and adopted grandma from India. When Sheela passed away, she left behind a wealth of memories and good cheer. This book is the result.

We want to thank Eda, Justin, and Ethan for bringing so much joy into our lives, and for supporting this project and sharing with us their own happy memories of the Zelda years. We also want to thank my sister Jil Greenbaum and my cousin Jim Fox for always being there for us, in the good times and the rough.

We want to give a special thank you to my agent Sandy Dijkstra and her marvelous team for loving the Zelda story, seeing its potential, and guiding us every step of the way. We also want to thank our editor Holly Rubino, our cover designer Diana Nuhn, our copy master Kristen Mellitt, and the whole wonderful team at Lyons Press for adopting the Zelda story and giving it a proper home.

Finally, Zelda and I offer a special salute to our pal, Jean-Claude Suarès. We provided the words and the story, but through the magic of his pen J.C. was able to bring Zelda right back to life with all her stylish dignity and panache. We and our readers thank you, J.C., for sharing with us your sense of whimsy and your very special creative spirit.

About the Author

Paul Chutkow has spent much of his life roaming the globe and writing about renowned artists, dreamers, and business pioneers. His many books include *Depardieu,* the biography of the French actor Gérard Depardieu; *Harvests of Joy,* the memoir of Robert Mondavi; and *Visa: The Power of an Idea,* the story of the men and women who created the Visa card, the ingenious little tool that has helped transform banking, commerce, and consumer life around the world.

Chutkow lives in an 1880s farmhouse overlooking the Napa Valley. His two sons, Justin and Ethan, are both international educators with a passion for travel, good food, and stray dogs of exceptional heart and soul.

636.7009
44361
Chutkow

Chutkow, Paul.

Zelda, the queen of
Paris

DUE DATE   22.95